W9-BEM-900

Windows® 95

SIMPLIFIED

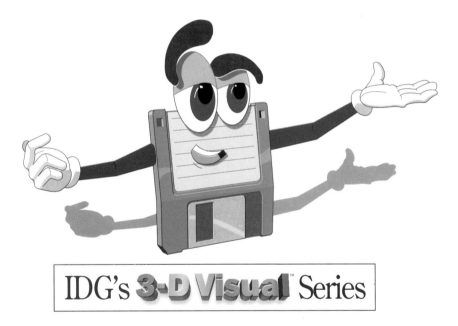

IDG's **3-D Visual**™ Series

IDG BOOKS

From
maranGraphics™

IDG Books Worldwide, Inc.
An International Data Group Company
Foster City, CA • Indianapolis • Chicago • Dallas

Windows® 95 Simplified

Published by
IDG Books Worldwide, Inc.
An International Data Group Company
919 E. Hillsdale Blvd., Suite 400
Foster City, CA 94404
(415) 655-3000

Library of Congress Catalog Card No.: 95-076879
ISBN: 1-56884-662-2
Printed in the United States of America
10 9 8

Distributed in the United States by IDG Books Worldwide, Inc.

Distributed by Computer and Technical Books in Miami, Florida, for South America and the Caribbean; by Longman Singapore in Singapore, Malaysia, Thailand, and Korea; by Toppan Co. Ltd. in Japan; by IDG Communications HK in Hong Kong; by WoodsLane Pty. Ltd. in Australia and New Zealand; and by Transworld Publishers Ltd. in the U.K. and Europe.

For general information on IDG Books in the U.S., including information on discounts and premiums, contact IDG Books at 800-762-2974 or 317-895-5200.

For U.S. Corporate Sales and quantity discounts, contact maranGraphics at 800-469-6616, ext. 206.

For information on international sales of IDG Books, contact Helen Saraceni at 415-655-3021, Fax number 415-655-3295.

For information on translations, contact Marc Jeffrey Mikulich, Director of Rights and Licensing, at IDG Books Worldwide. Fax Number 415-655-3295.

For sales inquiries and special prices for bulk quantities, write to the address above or call IDG Books Worldwide at 415-655-3000.

For information on using IDG Books in the classroom, or ordering examination copies, contact Jim Kelly at 800-434-2086.

Trademark Acknowledgments

©1995
maranGraphics, Inc.

The animated characters are the copyright of maranGraphics, Inc.

U.S. Corporate Sales	**U.S. Trade Sales**
Contact maranGraphics at (800) 469-6616, ext. 206 or Fax (905) 890-9434.	Contact IDG Books at (800) 434-3422 or (415) 655-3000.

About IDG Books Worldwide

Welcome to the world of IDG Books Worldwide.

IDG Books Worldwide, Inc., is a subsidiary of International Data Group, the world's largest publisher of business and computer-related information and the leading global provider of information services on information technology. IDG was founded more than 25 years ago and now employs more than 5,700 people worldwide. IDG publishes more than 200 computer publications in 63 countries (see listing below). Forty million people read one or more IDG publications each month.

Launched in 1990, IDG Books is today the fastest-growing publisher of computer and business books in the United States. We are proud to have received 3 awards from the Computer Press Association in recognition of editorial excellence, and our best-selling ...For Dummies series has more than 10 million copies in print with translations in more than 20 languages. IDG Books, through a recent joint venture with IDG's Hi-Tech Beijing, became the first U.S. publisher to publish a computer book in the People's Republic of China. In record time, IDG Books has become the first choice for millions of readers around the world who want to learn how to better manage their businesses.

Our mission is simple: Every IDG book is designed to bring extra value and skill-building instructions to the reader. Our books are written by experts who understand and care about our readers. The knowledge base of our editorial staff comes from years of experience in publishing, education, and journalism — experience which we use to produce books for the '90s. In short, we care about books, so we attract the best people. We devote special attention to details such as audience, interior design, use of icons, and illustrations. And because we use an efficient process of authoring, editing, and desktop publishing our books electronically, we can spend more time ensuring superior content and spend less time on the technicalities of making books.

You can count on our commitment to deliver high-quality books at competitive prices on topics customers want to read about. At IDG, we value quality, and we have been delivering quality for more than 25 years. You'll find no better book on a subject than an IDG book.

John Kilcullen
President and CEO
IDG Books Worldwide, Inc.

IDG Books Worldwide, Inc., is a subsidiary of International Data Group. The officers are Patrick J. McGovern, Founder and Board Chairman; Walter Boyd, President. International Data Group's publications include: ARGENTINA'S Computerworld Argentina, Infoworld Argentina; AUSTRALIA'S Computerworld Australia, Australian PC World, Australian Macworld, Network World, Mobile Business Australia, Reseller, IDG Sources; AUSTRIA'S Computerwelt Oesterreich, PC Test; BRAZIL'S Computerworld, Gamepro, Game Power, Mundo IBM, Mundo Unix, PC World, Super Game; BELGIUM'S Data News (CW) BULGARIA'S Computerworld Bulgaria, Ediworld, PC & Mac World Bulgaria, Network World Bulgaria; CANADA'S CIO Canada, Computerworld Canada, Graduate Computerworld, InfoCanada, Network World Canada; CHILE'S Computerworld Chile, Informatica; COLOMBIA'S Computerworld Colombia, PC World; CZECH REPUBLIC'S Computerworld, Elektronika, PC World; DENMARK'S Communications World, Computerworld Danmark, Macintosh Produktkatalog, Macworld Danmark, PC World Danmark, PC World Produktguide, Tech World, Windows World; ECUADOR'S PC World Ecuador; EGYPT'S Computerworld (CW) Middle East, PC World Middle East; FINLAND'S MikroPC, Tietoviikko, Tietoverkko; FRANCE'S Distributique, GOLDEN MAC, InfoPC, Languages & Systems, Le Guide du Monde Informatique, Le Monde Informatique, Telecoms & Reseaux; GERMANY'S Computerwoche, Computerwoche Focus, Computerwoche Extra, Computerwoche Karriere, Information Management, Macwelt, Netzwelt, PC Welt, PC Woche, Publish, Unit; GREECE'S Infoworld, PC Games; HUNGARY'S Computerworld SZT, PC World; HONG KONG'S Computerworld Hong Kong, PC World Hong Kong; INDIA'S Computers & Communications, IRELAND'S ComputerScope; ISRAEL'S Computerworld Israel, PC World Israel; ITALY'S Computerworld Italia, Lotus Magazine, Macworld Italia, Networking Italia, PC Shopping, PC World Italia; JAPAN'S Computerworld Today, Information Systems World, Macworld Japan, Nikkei Personal Computing, SunWorld Japan, Windows World; KENYA'S East African Computer News; KOREA'S Computerworld Korea, Macworld Korea, PC World Korea; MEXICO'S Compu Edicion, Compu Manufactura, Computacion/Punto de Venta, Computerworld Mexico, MacWorld, Mundo Unix, PC World, Windows; THE NETHERLANDS' Computer! Totaal, Computable (CW), LAN Magazine, MacWorld, Totaal "Windows"; NEW ZEALAND'S Computer Listings, Computerworld New Zealand, New Zealand PC World, Network World; NIGERIA'S PC World Africa; NORWAY'S Computerworld Norge, C/World, Lotusworld Norge, Macworld Norge, Networld, PC World Ekspress, PC World Norge, PC World Norges Produktguide, Publish& Multimedia World, Student Data, Unix World, Windowsworld; IDG Direct Response; PAKISTAN'S PC World Pakistan; PANAMA'S PC World Panama; PERU'S Computerworld Peru, PC World; PEOPLE'S REPUBLIC OF CHINA'S China Computerworld, China Infoworld, Electronics Today/Multimedia World, Electronics International, Electronic Product World, China Network World, PC and Communications Magazine, PC World China, Software World Magazine, Telecom Product World, IDG HIGH TECH BEIJING'S New Product World; IDG SHENZHEN'S Computer News Digest; PHILIPPINES' Computerworld Philippines, PC Digest (PCW); POLAND'S Computerworld Poland, PC World/Komputer; PORTUGAL'S Cerebro/PC World, Correio Informatico/Computerworld, Informatica & Comunicacoes Catalogo, MacIn, Nacional de Produtos, ROMANIA'S Computerworld, PC World; RUSSIA'S Computerworld-Moscow, Mir - PC, Sety; SINGAPORE'S Computerworld Southeast Asia, PC World Singapore; SLOVENIA'S Monitor Magazine; SOUTH AFRICA'S Computer Mail (CIO),Computing S A ,Network World S A , Software World; SPAIN'S Advanced Systems, Amiga World, Computerworld Espana, Communicaciones World, Macworld Espana, NeXTWORLD, Super Juegos Magazine (GamePro), PC World Espana, Publish; SWEDEN'S Attack, ComputerSweden, Corporate Computing, Natverk & Kommunikation, Macworld, Mikrodatorn, PC World, Publishing & Design (CAP), Datalngenjoren, Maxi Data,Windows World; SWITZERLAND'S Computerworld Schweiz, Macworld Schweiz, PC Tip; TAIWAN'S Computerworld Taiwan, PC World Taiwan; THAILAND'S Thai Computerworld; TURKEY'S Computerworld Monitor, Macworld Turkiye, PC World Turkiye; UKRAINE'S Computerworld; UNITED KINGDOM'S Computing /Computerworld, Connexion/Network World, Lotus Magazine, Macworld, Open Computing/Sunworld; UNITED STATES' Advanced Systems, AmigaWorld, Cable in the Classroom, CD Review, CIO, Computerworld, Digital Video, DOS Resource Guide, Electronic Entertainment Magazine, Federal Computer Week, Federal Integrator, GamePro, IDG Books, Infoworld, Infoworld Direct, Laser Event, Macworld, Multimedia World, Network World, PC Letter, PC World, PlayRight, Power PC World, Publish, SWATPro, Video Event; VENEZUELA'S Computerworld Venezuela, PC World; VIETNAM'S PC World Vietnam

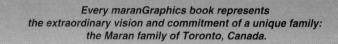

*Every maranGraphics book represents
the extraordinary vision and commitment of a unique family:
the Maran family of Toronto, Canada.*

Back Row (from left to right): Sherry Maran, Rob Maran, mG, Richard Maran,
Maxine Maran, Jill Maran.
Front Row (from left to right): mG, Judy Maran, Ruth Maran, mG.

Richard Maran is the company founder and its inspirational leader. He began maranGraphics over twenty years ago with a vision of a more efficient way to communicate a visual grammar that fuses text and graphics and allows readers to instantly grasp concepts.

Ruth Maran is the Author and Architect—a role Richard established that now bears Ruth's distinctive touch. She creates the words and visual structure that are the basis for the books.

Judy Maran is Senior Editor. She works with Ruth, Richard, and the highly talented maranGraphics illustrators, designers, and editors to transform Ruth's material into its final form.

Rob Maran is the Technical and Production Specialist. He makes sure the state-of-the-art technology used to create these books always performs as it should.

Sherry Maran manages the Reception, Order Desk, and any number of areas that require immediate attention and a helping hand.

Jill Maran is a jack-of-all-trades and dynamo who fills in anywhere she's needed anytime she's back from university.

Maxine Maran is the Business Manager and family sage. She maintains order in the business and family—and keeps everything running smoothly.

Oh, and there's **mG**. He's maranGraphics' spokesperson and, well, star. When you use a maranGraphics book, you'll see a lot of mG and his friends. They're just part of the family!

Credits

Author and Architect:
Ruth Maran

Technical Consultant:
Wendi Blouin Ewbank

Copy Developer & Editor:
Kelleigh Wing

Layout Designer:
Christie Van Duin

Illustrations:
Dave Ross
David de Haas
Tamara Poliquin

Editor:
Paul Lofthouse

Proofreaders:
Judy Maran
Catherine Manson

Indexer:
Carol Burbo

Post Production:
Robert Maran

Acknowledgments

Thanks to the dedicated staff of maranGraphics, including
David de Haas, Brad Hilderley, Chris K.C. Leung, Paul Lofthouse,
Catherine Manson, Jill Maran, Judy Maran, Maxine Maran,
Robert Maran, Sherry Maran, Russ Marini, Neil Mohan,
Tamara Poliquin, Dave Ross, Christie Van Duin, Nebojsa Visnjic
and Kelleigh Wing.

Finally, to Richard Maran who originated the easy-to-use graphic
format of this guide. Thank you for your inspiration and guidance.

TABLE OF CONTENTS

GETTING STARTED

WINDOWS BASICS

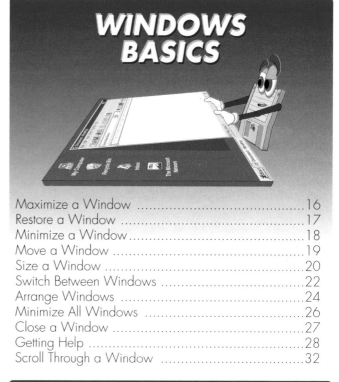

WORDPAD

PAINT

VIEW CONTENTS OF COMPUTER

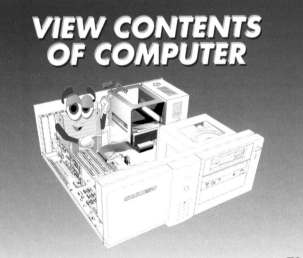

WORK WITH FILES AND FOLDERS

TABLE OF CONTENTS

USING WINDOWS EXPLORER

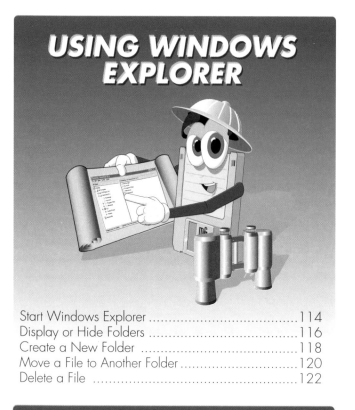

FAXING

CHANGE WINDOWS SETTINGS

THE MICROSOFT NETWORK

MAINTAIN YOUR COMPUTER

ELECTRONIC MAIL

BACK UP YOUR FILES

WINDOWS FUNCTIONS

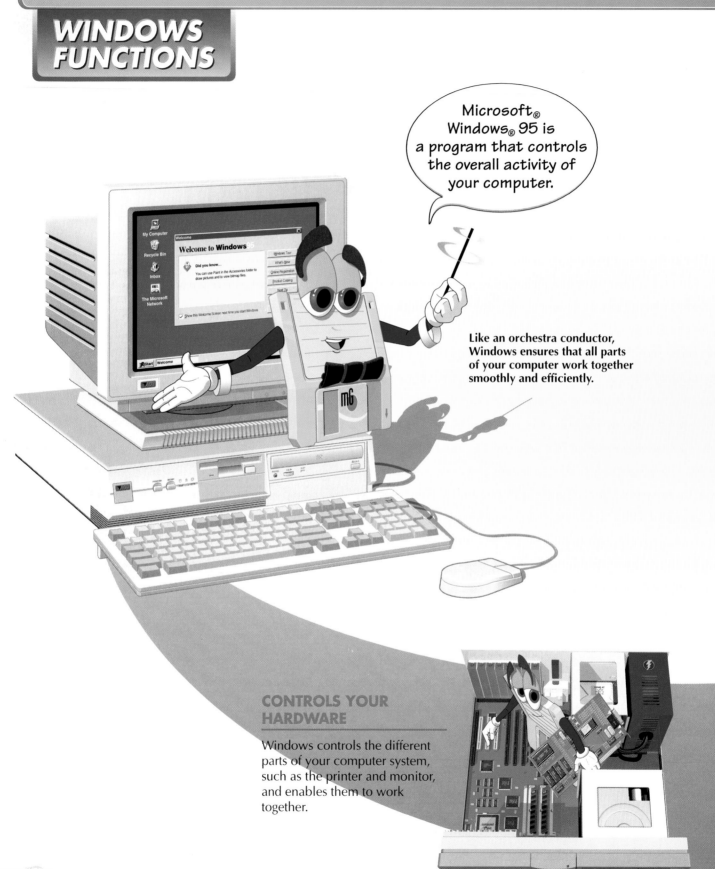

Microsoft® Windows® 95 is a program that controls the overall activity of your computer.

Like an orchestra conductor, Windows ensures that all parts of your computer work together smoothly and efficiently.

CONTROLS YOUR HARDWARE

Windows controls the different parts of your computer system, such as the printer and monitor, and enables them to work together.

RUNS YOUR PROGRAMS

Windows starts and operates programs, such as Microsoft Word and Lotus 1-2-3. Programs let you write letters, analyze numbers, manage finances, draw pictures and even play games.

Note: Windows comes with several useful programs. These include a word processor (WordPad) and a drawing program (Paint).

Our Budget

INCOME STATEMENT

REVENUE	$8,700	$11,500	$13,670	$33,870
Payroll	$3,850	$4,850	$5,250	$13,950
Rent	$1,750	$1,750	$1,750	$5,250
Supplies	$1,460	$1,590	$2,030	$5,900
TOTAL EXPENSES	$7,490	$8,560	$9,030	$25,100
INCOME	$1,210	$2,920	$4,640	$8,770

ORGANIZES YOUR INFORMATION

Windows provides ways to organize and manage files stored on your computer. You can use Windows to sort, copy, move, delete and view your files.

WINDOWS OVERVIEW

The Windows screen displays various items. The items that appear depend on how your computer is set up.

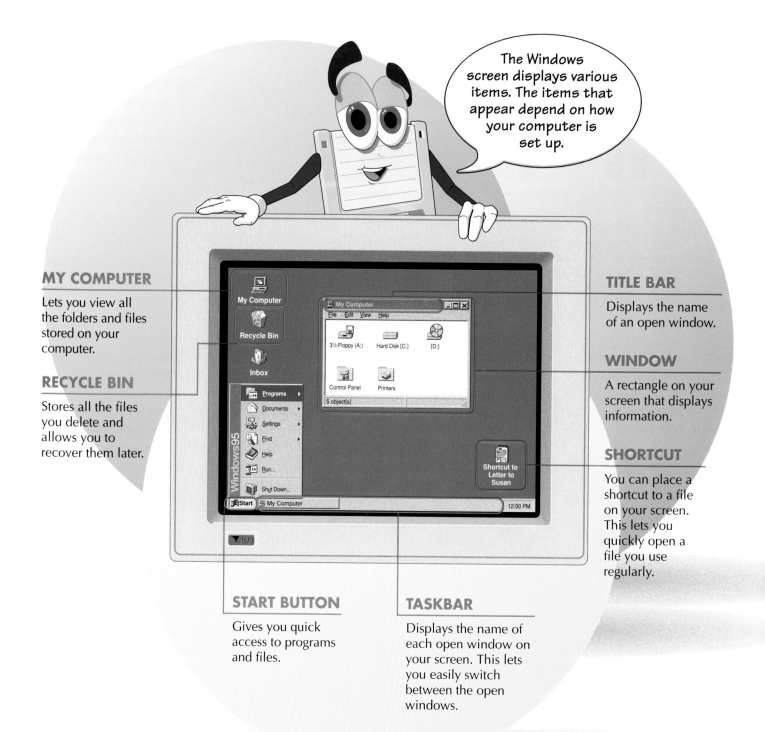

MY COMPUTER

Lets you view all the folders and files stored on your computer.

RECYCLE BIN

Stores all the files you delete and allows you to recover them later.

TITLE BAR

Displays the name of an open window.

WINDOW

A rectangle on your screen that displays information.

SHORTCUT

You can place a shortcut to a file on your screen. This lets you quickly open a file you use regularly.

START BUTTON

Gives you quick access to programs and files.

TASKBAR

Displays the name of each open window on your screen. This lets you easily switch between the open windows.

- Windows Functions
- Windows Overview
- Using the Mouse
- Start Windows
- Display the Date
- Using the Start Button
- Shut Down Windows

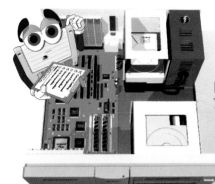

PLUG AND PLAY

Windows supports Plug and Play technology. This technology lets you add new features, such as CD-quality sound, to a computer without complex and time-consuming installation procedures.

EXPLORER

Like a map, Windows Explorer shows you the location of each folder and file on your computer. This helps you manage your information.

FILENAMES

Windows lets you use up to 255 characters to name a file.

THE MICROSOFT NETWORK

Like CompuServe or Prodigy, The Microsoft Network is an online information service. It provides data from sources around the world and lets you communicate with other people connected to the service.

The Microsoft Network also lets you connect to the Internet. The Internet provides a vast amount of information, news and advice and now reaches over thirty million people.

The mouse is a hand-held device that lets you select and move items on your screen.

USING THE MOUSE

◆ Hold the mouse as shown in the diagram. Use your thumb and two rightmost fingers to move the mouse while your two remaining fingers press the mouse buttons.

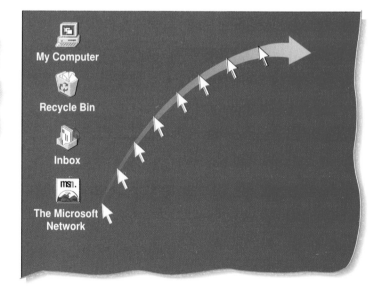

My Computer

Recycle Bin

Inbox

The Microsoft Network

◆ When you move the mouse on your desk, the mouse pointer ⍩ on your screen moves in the same direction. The mouse pointer assumes different shapes (examples: ⍩, I), depending on its location on your screen and the task you are performing.

PARTS OF THE MOUSE

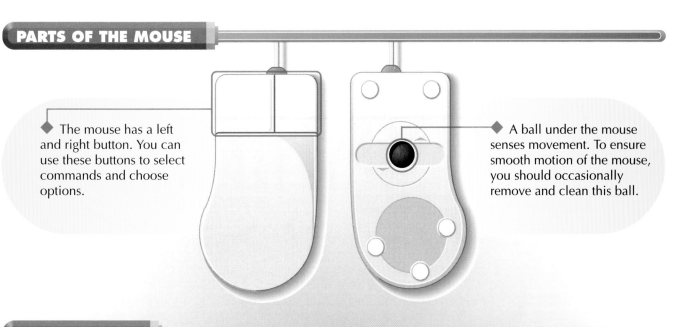

◆ The mouse has a left and right button. You can use these buttons to select commands and choose options.

◆ A ball under the mouse senses movement. To ensure smooth motion of the mouse, you should occasionally remove and clean this ball.

MOUSE TERMS

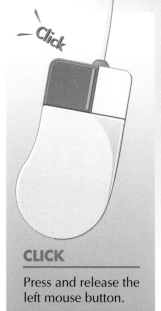

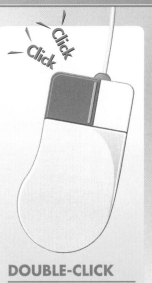

CLICK

Press and release the left mouse button.

DOUBLE-CLICK

Quickly press and release the left mouse button twice.

DRAG AND DROP

When the mouse pointer is over an object on your screen, press and hold down the left mouse button. Still holding down the button, move the mouse to where you want to place the object and then release the button.

Windows provides an easy, graphical way for you to use your computer.

START WINDOWS

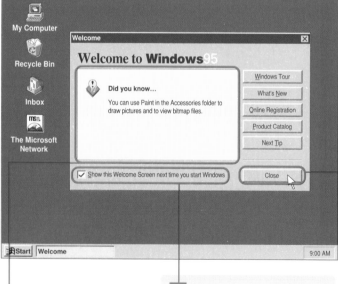

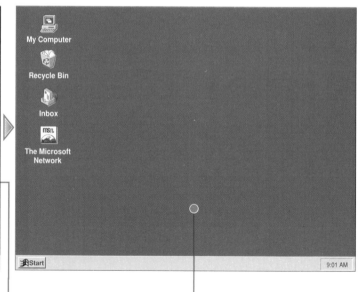

◆ When you start Windows, the **Welcome** dialog box appears. It displays a tip about using Windows.

1 If you do not want this dialog box to appear every time you start Windows, move the mouse ⟍ over this option and then press the left button (☑ changes to ☐).

2 To close the dialog box, move the mouse ⟍ over **Close** and then press the left button.

◆ The dialog box disappears and you can clearly view your desktop. The **desktop** is the background area of your screen.

- Windows Functions
- Windows Overview
- Using the Mouse
- **Start Windows**

- **Display the Date**
- Using the Start Button
- Shut Down Windows

You can easily display the date on your screen.

DISPLAY THE DATE

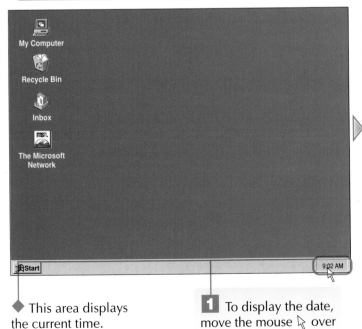

◆ This area displays the current time.

1 To display the date, move the mouse over this area.

◆ After a few seconds, the date appears.

Note: If Windows displays the wrong date or time, you can change the date or time set in your computer. For more information, refer to page 126.

USING THE START BUTTON

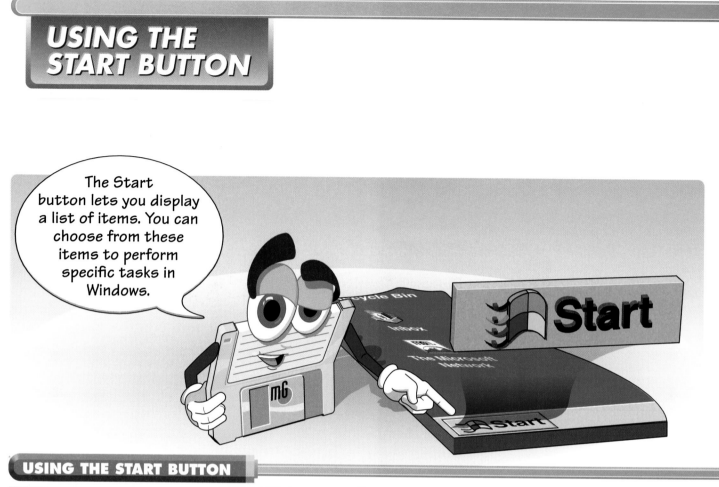

The Start button lets you display a list of items. You can choose from these items to perform specific tasks in Windows.

USING THE START BUTTON

1 Move the mouse ⌖ over **Start** and then press the left button.

◆ A menu appears.

2 To select an item that displays an arrow (▸), move the mouse ⌖ over the item (example: **Programs**). Another menu appears.

◆ To select an item that does not display an arrow, move the mouse ⌖ over the item (example: **Help**) and then press the left button.

- Windows Functions
- Windows Overview
- Using the Mouse
- Start Windows
- Display the Date
- **Using the Start Button**
- Shut Down Windows

♦ If you select an item that displays an arrow (▸), another menu appears on your screen.

♦ If you select an item that does not display an arrow, the window that lets you perform the task appears on your screen.

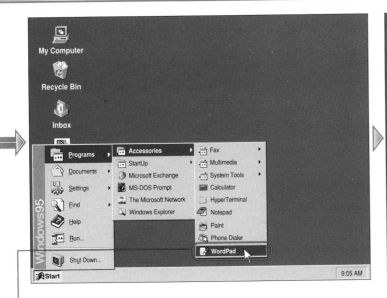

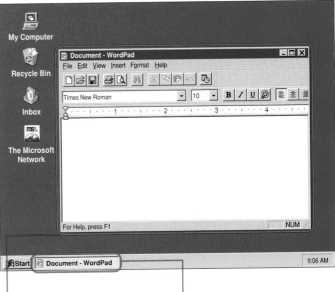

3 Repeat step **2** until you see the item you want to select (example: **WordPad**).

4 Move the mouse ⟍ over the item and then press the left button.

*Note: To close the **Start** menu without selecting an item, move the mouse ⟍ outside the menu area and then press the left button.*

♦ In this example, the **WordPad** window appears on your screen.

Note: For information on using WordPad, refer to the WordPad chapter, starting on page 36.

♦ The **taskbar** displays a button for the open window.

Note: To close a window to remove it from your screen, refer to page 27.

SHUT DOWN WINDOWS

It's now safe to turn off your computer.

When you finish using Windows, you can shut down the program.

SHUT DOWN WINDOWS

1 Move the mouse ⌖ over **Start** and then press the left button.

2 Move the mouse ⌖ over **Shut Down** and then press the left button.

IMPORTANT!

To avoid damaging your information, you must shut down Windows before turning off your computer.

◆ The **Shut Down Windows** dialog box appears.

3 To shut down your computer, move the mouse ⬞ over **Yes** and then press the left button.

◆ You can now safely turn off your computer.

WINDOWS BASICS

Maximize a Window

Restore a Window

Minimize a Window

Move a Window

Size a Window

Switch Between Windows

Arrange Windows

Minimize All Windows

Close a Window

Getting Help

Scroll Through a Window

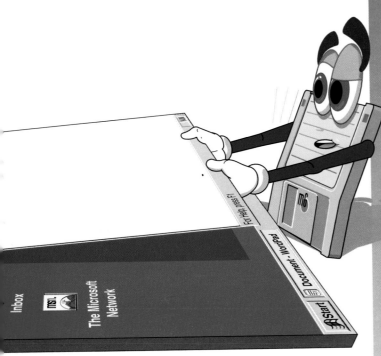

MAXIMIZE A WINDOW

RESTORE A WINDOW

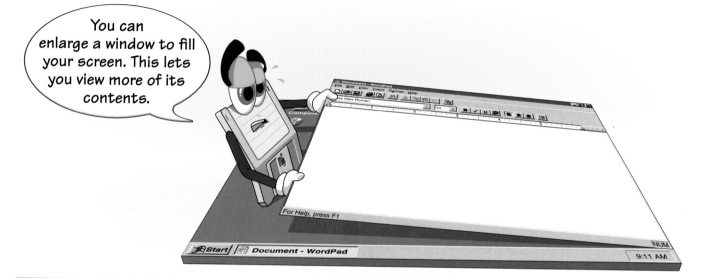

You can enlarge a window to fill your screen. This lets you view more of its contents.

MAXIMIZE A WINDOW

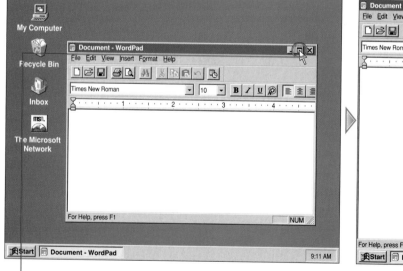

1 Move the mouse ⌀ over 🔲 in the window you want to enlarge and then press the left button.

Note: To display the WordPad window, refer to page 36.

◆ The window fills your screen.

- **Maximize a Window**
- **Restore a Window**
- Minimize a Window
- Move a Window
- Size a Window
- Switch Between Windows
- Arrange Windows
- Minimize All Windows
- Close a Window
- Getting Help
- Scroll Through a Window

You can return a maximized window to its previous size. This lets you view information hidden behind the window.

RESTORE A WINDOW

1 Move the mouse ⌖ over 🗗 in the window you want to restore and then press the left button.

Note: Only maximized windows display the Restore button (🗗).

◆ The window returns to its previous size.

If you are not using a window, you can minimize the window to remove it from your screen. You can redisplay the window at any time.

MINIMIZE A WINDOW

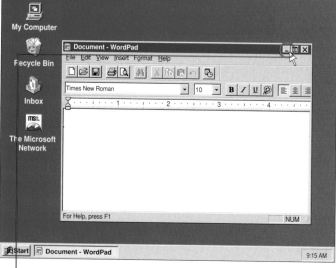

1 Move the mouse ⩗ over ⬓ in the window you want to minimize and then press the left button.

◆ The window disappears.

2 To redisplay the window on your screen, move the mouse ⩗ over its button on the taskbar and then press the left button.

- Maximize a Window
- Restore a Window
- *Minimize a Window*
- *Move a Window*

- Size a Window
- Switch Between Windows
- Arrange Windows
- Minimize All Windows

- Close a Window
- Getting Help
- Scroll Through a Window

If a window covers items on your screen, you can move the window to a different location.

MOVE A WINDOW

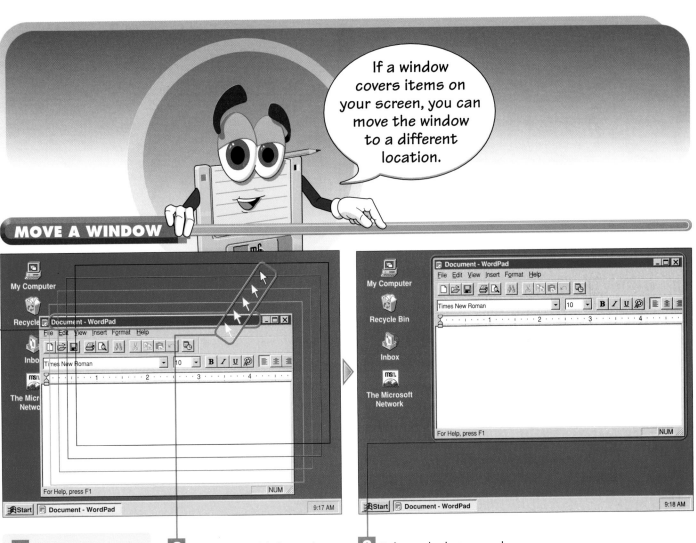

1 Move the mouse ▷ over the title bar of the window you want to move.

2 Press and hold down the left button as you drag the mouse ▷ to where you want to place the window.

◆ An outline of the window indicates the new location.

3 Release the button and the window moves to the new location.

SIZE A WINDOW

You can easily change the size of a window displayed on your screen.

- Enlarging a window lets you view more of its contents.
- Reducing a window lets you view items covered by the window.

SIZE A WINDOW

1 Move the mouse ⬚ over an edge of the window you want to size and ⬚ changes to ↕ .

2 Press and hold down the left button.

3 Still holding down the button, drag the mouse ↕ until the outline of the window displays the size you want.

- Maximize a Window
- Restore a Window
- Minimize a Window
- Move a Window

- **Size a Window**
- Switch Between Windows
- Arrange Windows
- Minimize All Windows

- Close a Window
- Getting Help
- Scroll Through a Window

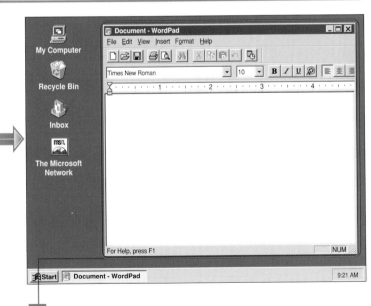

4 Release the button and the window changes to the new size.

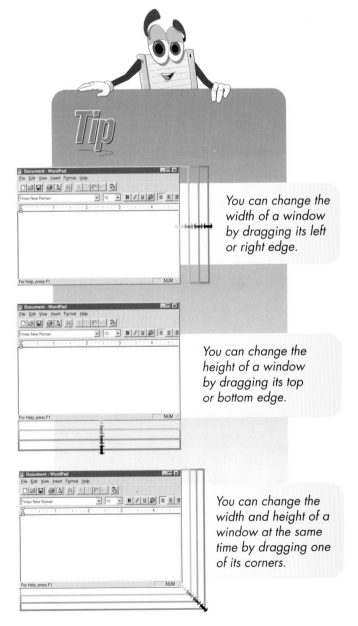

You can change the width of a window by dragging its left or right edge.

You can change the height of a window by dragging its top or bottom edge.

You can change the width and height of a window at the same time by dragging one of its corners.

You can easily switch between all of the windows you have opened. This lets you clearly view the window you want to work with.

SWITCH BETWEEN WINDOWS

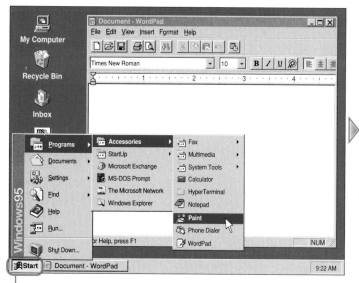

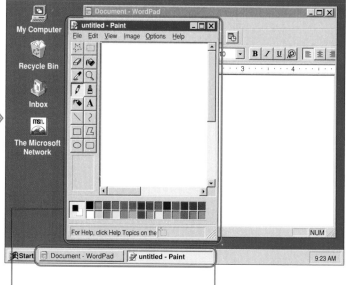

◆ In this example, the Start button was used to open the **Paint** window.

Note: To use the Start button, refer to page 10.

◆ You can only work in one window at a time. The active window (example: **Paint**) appears in front of all other windows.

Note: Think of each window as a separate piece of paper. When you open a window, you are placing a new piece of paper on your screen.

◆ The taskbar displays a button for each open window on your screen.

- Maximize a Window
- Restore a Window
- Minimize a Window
- Move a Window
- Size a Window
- **Switch Between Windows**
- Arrange Windows
- Minimize All Windows
- Close a Window
- Getting Help
- Scroll Through a Window

Tip

You can also use your keyboard to quickly switch between the open windows on your screen.

Document - WordPad

1 *Press and hold down* Alt *on your keyboard.*

2 *Still holding down* Alt, *press* Tab *until the name of the window you want to work with appears. Then release* Alt.

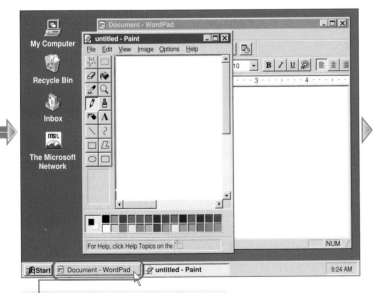

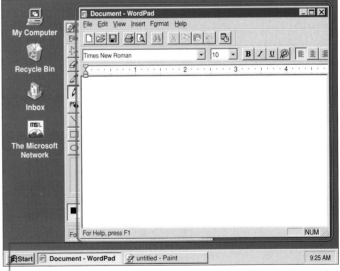

1 To move the window you want to work with to the front, move the mouse ⟍ over its button on the taskbar (example: **WordPad**) and then press the left button.

◆ The window appears in front of all other windows. This lets you clearly view its contents.

ARRANGE WINDOWS

If you have several windows open, some of them may be hidden from view. The Cascade command lets you display your open windows one on top of the other.

CASCADE WINDOWS

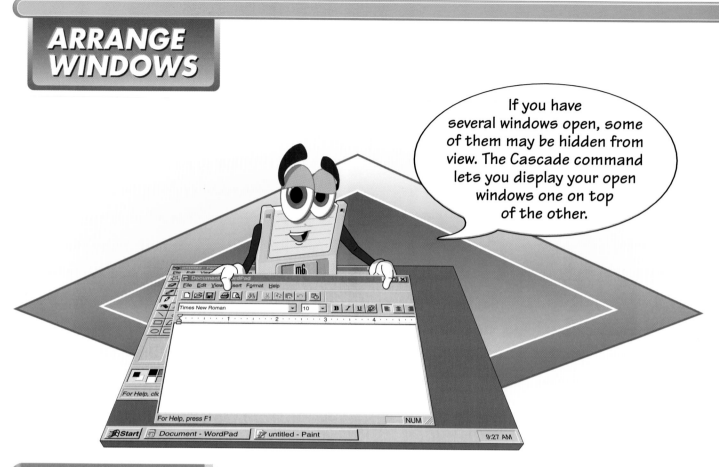

1 Move the mouse ⬚ over an empty area on the taskbar and then press the **right** button. A menu appears.

2 Move the mouse ⬚ over **Cascade** and then press the left button.

◆ The windows neatly overlap each other.

- Maximize a Window
- Restore a Window
- Minimize a Window
- Move a Window

- Size a Window
- Switch Between Windows
- **Arrange Windows**
- Minimize All Windows

- Close a Window
- Getting Help
- Scroll Through a Window

You can use the Tile command to view the contents of all your open windows.

TILE WINDOWS

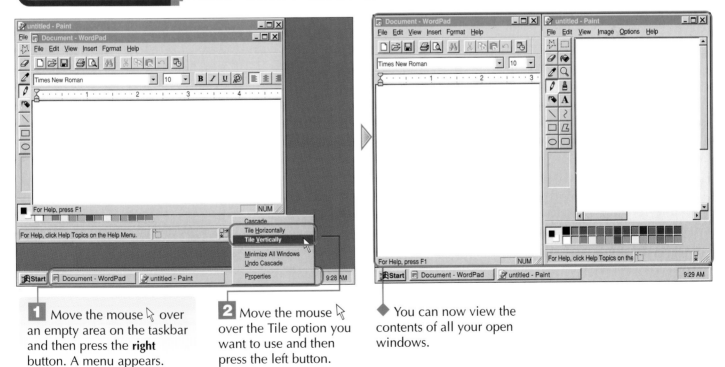

1 Move the mouse ⬚ over an empty area on the taskbar and then press the **right** button. A menu appears.

2 Move the mouse ⬚ over the Tile option you want to use and then press the left button.

◆ You can now view the contents of all your open windows.

MINIMIZE ALL WINDOWS

CLOSE A WINDOW

You can minimize all your open windows to remove them from your screen. You can redisplay a window at any time.

MINIMIZE ALL WINDOWS

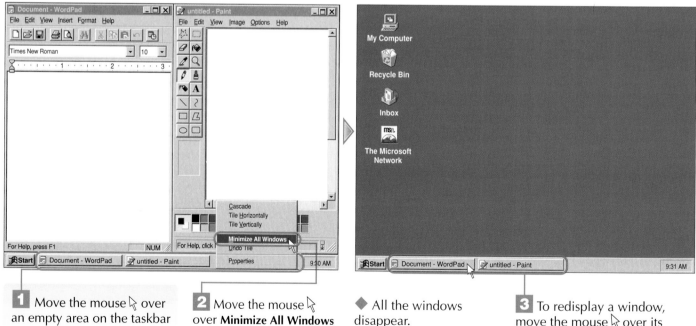

1 Move the mouse ⬚ over an empty area on the taskbar and then press the **right** button. A menu appears.

2 Move the mouse ⬚ over **Minimize All Windows** and then press the left button.

◆ All the windows disappear.

3 To redisplay a window, move the mouse ⬚ over its button on the taskbar (example: **WordPad**) and then press the left button.

- Maximize a Window
- Restore a Window
- Minimize a Window
- Move a Window

- Size a Window
- Switch Between Windows
- Arrange Windows
- **Minimize All Windows**

- **Close a Window**
- Getting Help
- Scroll Through a Window

When you finish working with a window, you can close the window to remove it from your screen.

CLOSE A WINDOW

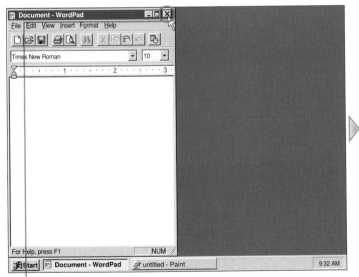

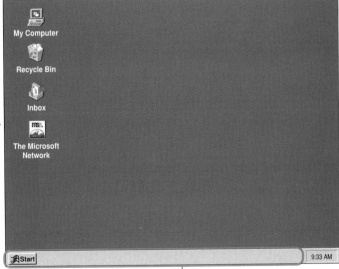

1 Move the mouse ⌖ over ⌧ in the window you want to close and then press the left button.

◆ The window disappears from your screen.

◆ The button for the window disappears from the taskbar.

Note: In this example, the Paint window was also closed.

If you do not know how to perform a task, you can use the Help feature to obtain information.

1 Move the mouse over **Start** and then press the left button.

2 Move the mouse over **Help** and then press the left button.

◆ The **Help Topics** window appears.

3 To display the help index, move the mouse over the **Index** tab and then press the left button.

◆ This area displays a list of all the available help topics.

- Maximize a Window
- Restore a Window
- Minimize a Window
- Move a Window

- Size a Window
- Switch Between Windows
- Arrange Windows
- Minimize All Windows

- Close a Window
- **Getting Help**
- Scroll Through a Window

Tip

There are three ways to find information in the Help Topics dialog box.

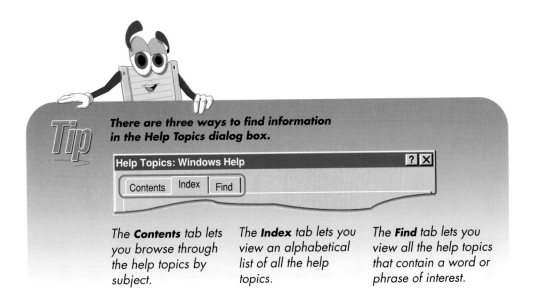

The **Contents** tab lets you browse through the help topics by subject.

The **Index** tab lets you view an alphabetical list of all the help topics.

The **Find** tab lets you view all the help topics that contain a word or phrase of interest.

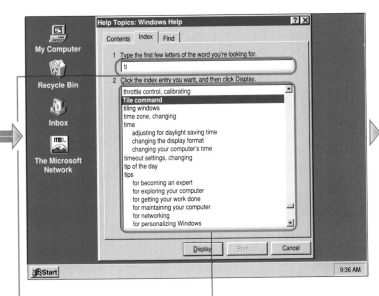

4 Move the mouse I over this area and then press the left button.

5 Type the first few letters of the topic of interest (example: **ti** for **time**).

◆ This area displays topics beginning with the letters you typed.

Note: To browse through the topics, use the scroll bar. For more information, refer to page 32.

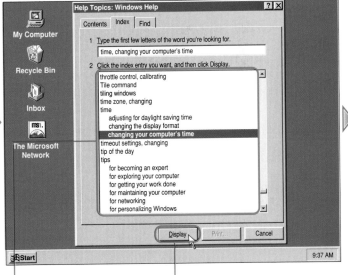

6 Move the mouse ⌖ over the topic you want information on and then press the left button.

7 Move the mouse ⌖ over **Display** and then press the left button.

CONTINUED

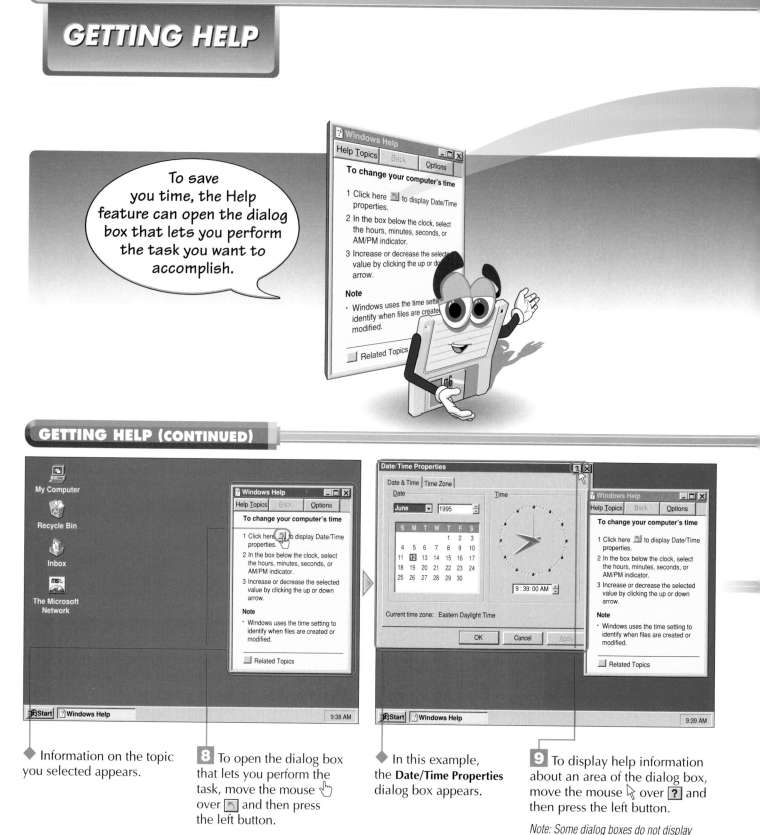

◆ Information on the topic you selected appears.

8 To open the dialog box that lets you perform the task, move the mouse ⛶ over 🔲 and then press the left button.

Note: Some help topics do not display the 🔲 button.

◆ In this example, the **Date/Time Properties** dialog box appears.

9 To display help information about an area of the dialog box, move the mouse ⬉ over ? and then press the left button.

Note: Some dialog boxes do not display the ? button.

- Maximize a Window
- Restore a Window
- Minimize a Window
- Move a Window
- Size a Window
- Switch Between Windows
- Arrange Windows
- Minimize All Windows
- Close a Window
- **Getting Help**
- Scroll Through a Window

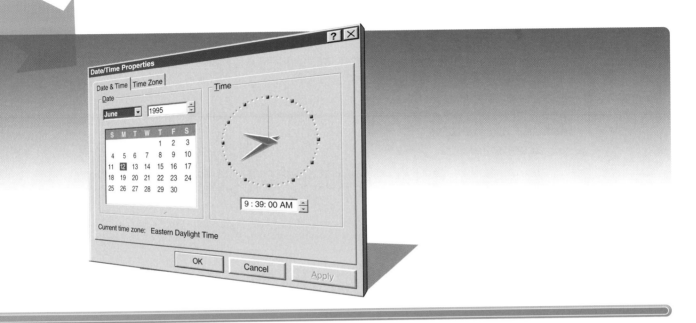

10 Move the mouse ▷? over an area of interest and then press the left button.

◆ A description of the area appears.

11 To hide the description, press the left button.

12 To close the **Date/Time Properties** dialog box, move the mouse ▷ over ✕ and then press the left button.

13 To close the **Windows Help** window, move the mouse ▷ over ✕ and then press the left button.

SCROLL THROUGH A WINDOW

A scroll bar lets you browse through information in a window. This is useful when a window is not large enough to display all the information it contains.

SCROLL DOWN

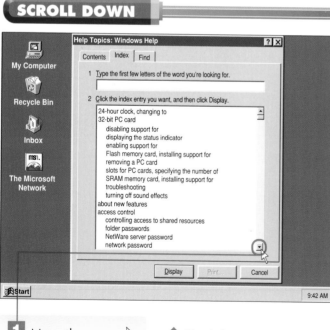

1 Move the mouse ⍾ over ▾ and then press the left button.

◆ The information moves up one line, displaying a new line of information at the bottom of the window.

SCROLL UP

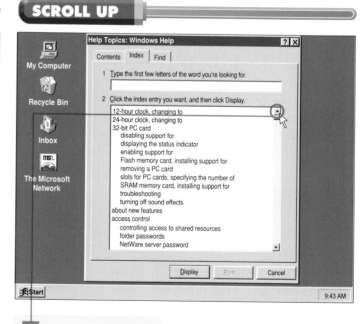

1 Move the mouse ⍾ over ▴ and then press the left button.

◆ The information moves down one line, displaying a new line of information at the top of the window.

- Maximize a Window
- Restore a Window
- Minimize a Window
- Move a Window
- Size a Window
- Switch Between Windows
- Arrange Windows
- Minimize All Windows
- Close a Window
- Getting Help
- **Scroll Through a Window**

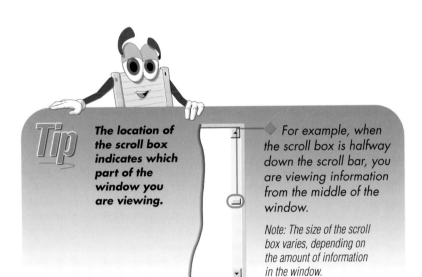

Tip

The location of the scroll box indicates which part of the window you are viewing.

For example, when the scroll box is halfway down the scroll bar, you are viewing information from the middle of the window.

Note: The size of the scroll box varies, depending on the amount of information in the window.

SCROLL TO ANY POSITION

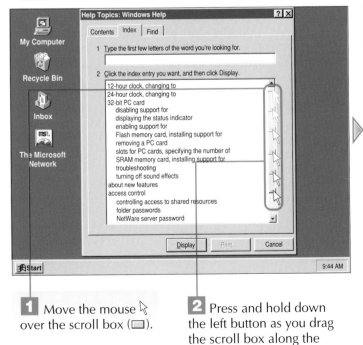

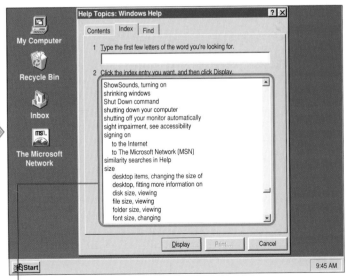

1 Move the mouse ▷ over the scroll box (▭).

2 Press and hold down the left button as you drag the scroll box along the scroll bar.

3 Release the button when you see the information you want.

WORDPAD

Start WordPad

Enter Text

Save a Document

Exit WordPad

Open a Document

Print a Document

Select Text

Change Font Size

Change Font Type

Edit Text

Move Text

Bold, Italic and Underline

Change Alignment of Text

WordPad helps you create professional-looking documents, such as letters and memos.

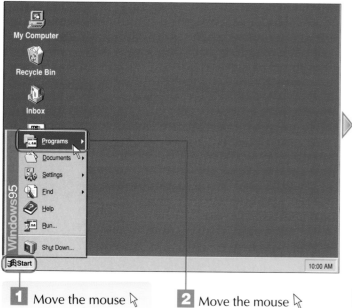

START WORDPAD

1 Move the mouse over **Start** and then press the left button.

2 Move the mouse over **Programs**.

3 Move the mouse over **Accessories**.

4 Move the mouse over **WordPad** and then press the left button.

- Start WordPad
- Enter Text
- Save a Document
- Exit WordPad
- Open a Document
- Print a Document
- Select Text
- Change Font Size
- Change Font Type
- Edit Text
- Move Text
- Bold, Italic and Underline
- Change Alignment of Text

When typing text in a document, you do not need to press **Enter** at the end of a line. WordPad automatically moves the text to the next line.

ENTER TEXT

◆ The **WordPad** window appears.

5 To enlarge the **WordPad** window to fill your screen, move the mouse ⤵ over ☐ and then press the left button.

◆ The flashing line in the window is called the insertion point. It indicates where the text you type will appear.

1 Type the first line of text.

2 To start a new paragraph, press **Enter** twice.

3 Type the remaining text.

◆ Press **Enter** only when you want to start a new line or paragraph.

You should save your document to store it for future use. This lets you later retrieve the document for reviewing or editing purposes.

SAVE A DOCUMENT

1 Move the mouse ⌖ over 🖫 and then press the left button.

◆ The **Save As** dialog box appears.

*Note: If you previously saved your document, the **Save As** dialog box will not appear, since you have already named the document.*

2 Type a name for your document (example: **my letter**).

*Note: You can use up to 255 characters to name a document. The name cannot contain the characters \ ? : * " < > or I.*

3 Move the mouse ⌖ over **Save** and then press the left button.

- Start WordPad
- Enter Text
- **Save a Document**
- **Exit WordPad**
- Open a Document

- Print a Document
- Select Text
- Change Font Size
- Change Font Type
- Edit Text

- Move Text
- Bold, Italic and Underline
- Change Alignment of Text

When you finish using WordPad, you can exit the program.

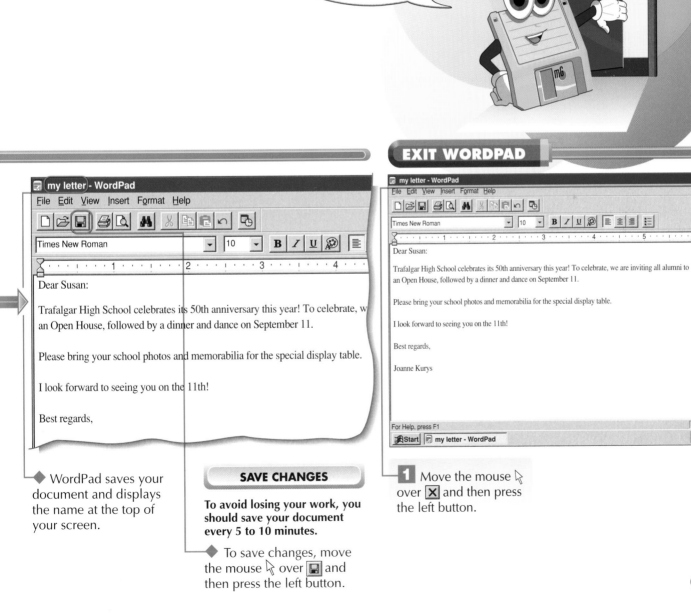

EXIT WORDPAD

◆ WordPad saves your document and displays the name at the top of your screen.

SAVE CHANGES

To avoid losing your work, you should save your document every 5 to 10 minutes.

◆ To save changes, move the mouse ⬚ over 🖫 and then press the left button.

1 Move the mouse ⬚ over ✕ and then press the left button.

You can open a saved document and display it on your screen. This lets you view and make changes to the document.

◆ To start **WordPad**, refer to page 36.

1 Move the mouse ⌖ over 🖿 and then press the left button.

◆ The **Open** dialog box appears.

2 Move the mouse ⌖ over the name of the document you want to open (example: **my letter**) and then press the left button.

Note: If you cannot find the document you want to open, refer to page 108 to find the document.

3 Move the mouse ⌖ over **Open** and then press the left button.

- Start WordPad
- Enter Text
- Save a Document
- Exit WordPad
- **Open a Document**

- Print a Document
- Select Text
- Change Font Size
- Change Font Type
- Edit Text

- Move Text
- Bold, Italic and Underline
- Change Alignment of Text

IMPORTANT!

WordPad only lets you work with one document at a time. If you are currently working with a document, save the document before opening another.

Note: For information on saving a document, refer to page 38.

DOCUMENT 1

The File menu displays the names of the last four documents you opened.

Note: In this example, only one document has been opened.

To open one of these documents:

1 Move the mouse over **File** and then press the left button.

2 Move the mouse over the name of the document you want to open and then press the left button.

◆ WordPad opens the document and displays it on your screen. You can now review and make changes to the document.

You can produce a paper copy of the document displayed on your screen.

PRINT A DOCUMENT

1 Move the mouse ⍾ over **File** and then press the left button.

2 Move the mouse ⍾ over **Print** and then press the left button.

◆ The **Print** dialog box appears.

3 To print the document, move the mouse ⍾ over **OK** and then press the left button.

- Start WordPad
- Enter Text
- Save a Document
- Exit WordPad
- Open a Document

- **Print a Document**
- **Select Text**
- Change Font Size
- Change Font Type
- Edit Text

- Move Text
- Bold, Italic and Underline
- Change Alignment of Text

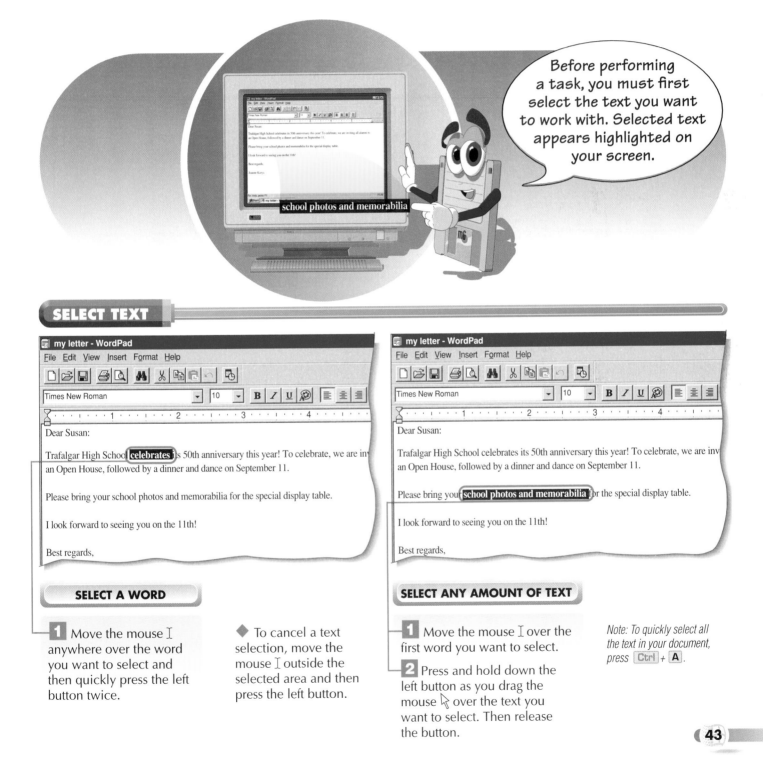

> Before performing a task, you must first select the text you want to work with. Selected text appears highlighted on your screen.

SELECT TEXT

SELECT A WORD

1 Move the mouse I anywhere over the word you want to select and then quickly press the left button twice.

◆ To cancel a text selection, move the mouse I outside the selected area and then press the left button.

SELECT ANY AMOUNT OF TEXT

1 Move the mouse I over the first word you want to select.

2 Press and hold down the left button as you drag the mouse ⌖ over the text you want to select. Then release the button.

Note: To quickly select all the text in your document, press **Ctrl** + **A**.

You can increase or decrease the size of text in your document.

8 point
12 point
14 point
18 point
24 point

WordPad measures the size of text in points. There are approximately 72 points in one inch.

- Larger text is easier to read.
- Smaller text lets you fit more information on one page.

CHANGE FONT SIZE

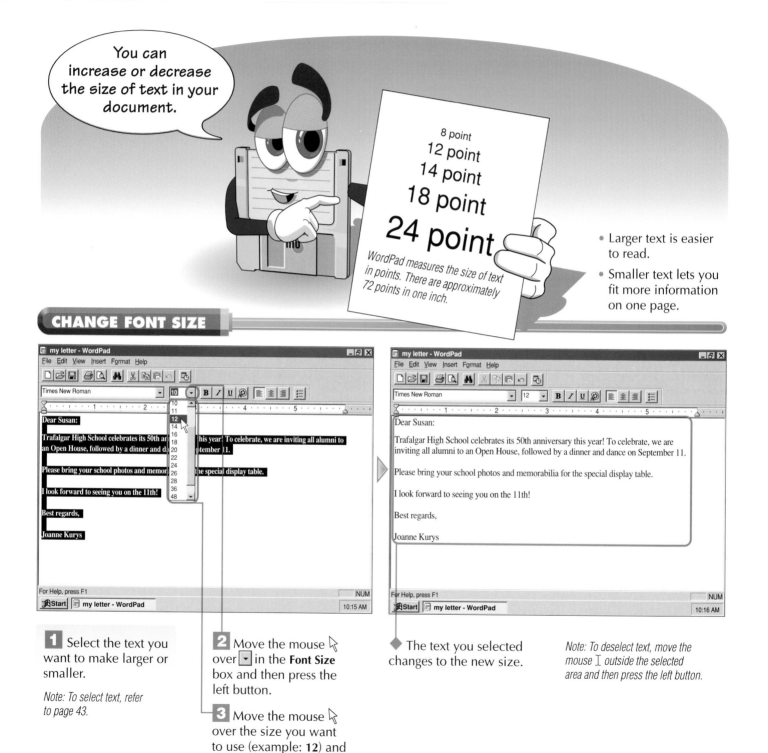

1 Select the text you want to make larger or smaller.

Note: To select text, refer to page 43.

2 Move the mouse ⤷ over ▾ in the **Font Size** box and then press the left button.

3 Move the mouse ⤷ over the size you want to use (example: **12**) and then press the left button.

◆ The text you selected changes to the new size.

Note: To deselect text, move the mouse I outside the selected area and then press the left button.

44

- Start WordPad
- Enter Text
- Save a Document
- Exit WordPad
- Open a Document

- Print a Document
- Select Text
- Change Font Size
- Change Font Type
- Edit Text

- Move Text
- Bold, Italic and Underline
- Change Alignment of Text

> You can enhance the appearance of your document by changing the design of characters.

CHANGE FONT TYPE

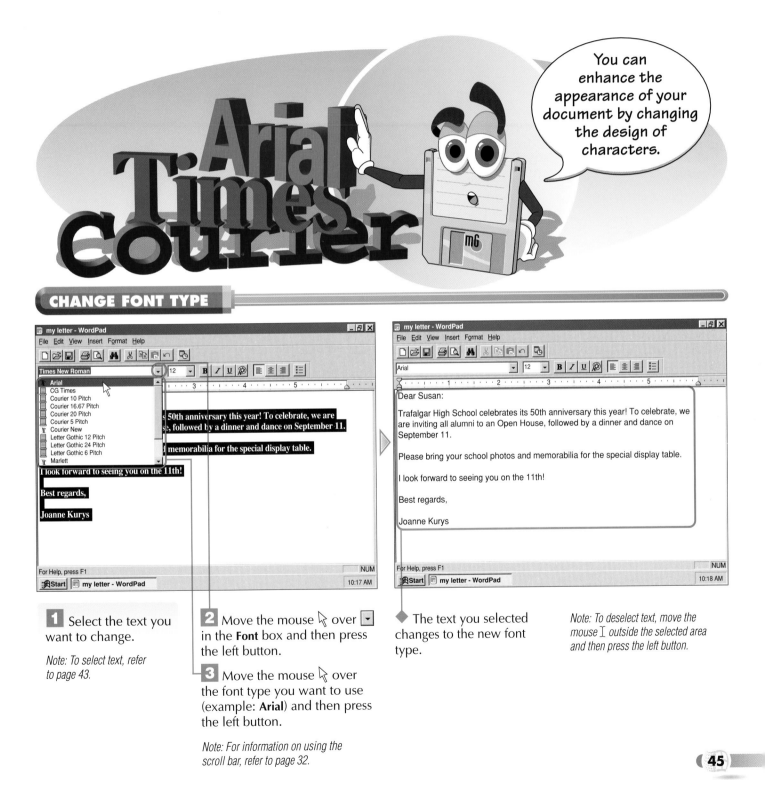

1 Select the text you want to change.

Note: To select text, refer to page 43.

2 Move the mouse ⬡ over ▾ in the **Font** box and then press the left button.

3 Move the mouse ⬡ over the font type you want to use (example: **Arial**) and then press the left button.

Note: For information on using the scroll bar, refer to page 32.

◆ The text you selected changes to the new font type.

Note: To deselect text, move the mouse Ⅰ outside the selected area and then press the left button.

EDIT TEXT

You can easily add new text to your document and remove text you no longer need.

my letter - WordPad

File Edit View Insert Format Help

Arial   12   **B** *I* U

Dear Susan:

Trafalgar High School celebrates its 50th anniversary this year!
are inviting all alumni to an Open House, followed by a dinner a
September 11.

Please bring your school photos and memorabilia for the specia

I look forward to seeing you on the 11th!

Best regards,

1 Move the mouse I to where you want to insert the new text and then press the left button.

my letter - WordPad

File Edit View Insert Format Help

Arial   12   **B** *I* U

Dear Susan:

Trafalgar High School celebrates its 50th anniversary this year!
are inviting all alumni (and students) to an Open House, followed
dance on September 11.

Please bring your school photos and memorabilia for the specia

I look forward to seeing you on the 11th!

Best regards,

2 Type the text you want to insert.

3 To insert a blank space, press the **Spacebar**.

Note: The words to the right of the new text move forward.

- Start WordPad
- Enter Text
- Save a Document
- Exit WordPad
- Open a Document

- Print a Document
- Select Text
- Change Font Size
- Change Font Type
- **Edit Text**

- Move Text
- Bold, Italic and Underline
- Change Alignment of Text

Delete a character|s

Delete a character|

DELETE A CHARACTER

1 Move the mouse I to the left of the character you want to delete and then press the left button.

2 Press Delete on your keyboard.

DELETE TEXT

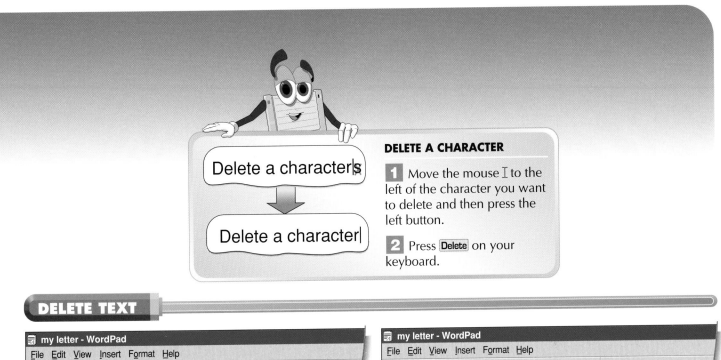

my letter - WordPad

File   Edit   View   Insert   Format   Help

Arial   12   B *I* U

Dear Susan:

Trafalgar High School celebrates its 50th anniversary this year! are inviting all alumni and students to an Open House, followed dance on September 11.

Please bring your school photos **and memorabilia** or the specia

I look forward to seeing you on the 11th!

Best regards,

my letter - WordPad

File   Edit   View   Insert   Format   Help

Arial   12   B *I* U

Dear Susan:

Trafalgar High School celebrates its 50th anniversary this year! are inviting all alumni and students to an Open House, followed dance on September 11.

Please bring your school photos for the special display table.

I look forward to seeing you on the 11th!

Best regards,

1 Select the text you want to delete.

Note: To select text, refer to page 43.

2 Press Delete on your keyboard to remove the text.

You can reorganize your document by moving text from one location to another.

1 Select the text you want to move.

Note: To select text, refer to page 43.

2 Move the mouse ⌖ over ✂ and then press the left button.

- Start WordPad
- Enter Text
- Save a Document
- Exit WordPad
- Open a Document

- Print a Document
- Select Text
- Change Font Size
- Change Font Type
- Edit Text

- **Move Text**
- Bold, Italic and Underline
- Change Alignment of Text

Tip

You can also place a copy of text in a different location.

1 To copy text, perform steps **1** to **4** below, selecting in step **2** .

◆ The text you selected disappears from your screen.

3 Move the mouse I over the location where you want to place the text and then press the left button.

4 Move the mouse over 🔳 and then press the left button.

◆ The text appears in the new location.

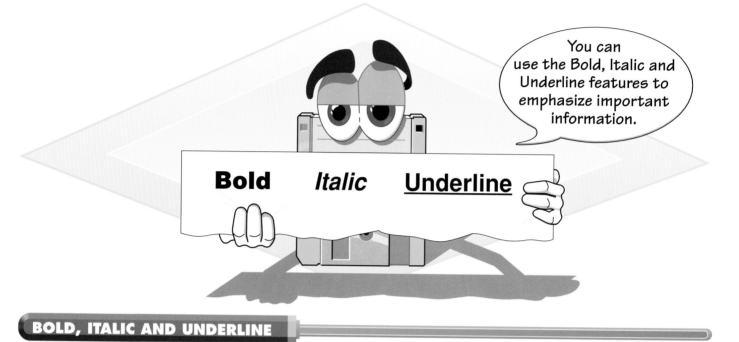

You can use the Bold, Italic and Underline features to emphasize important information.

Bold   *Italic*   <u>Underline</u>

BOLD, ITALIC AND UNDERLINE

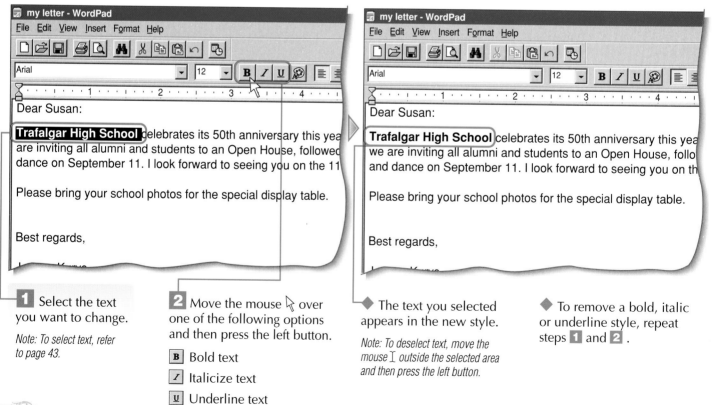

1 Select the text you want to change.

Note: To select text, refer to page 43.

2 Move the mouse ⬚ over one of the following options and then press the left button.

B Bold text

I Italicize text

<u>U</u> Underline text

◆ The text you selected appears in the new style.

Note: To deselect text, move the mouse ⌶ outside the selected area and then press the left button.

◆ To remove a bold, italic or underline style, repeat steps **1** and **2**.

- Start WordPad
- Enter Text
- Save a Document
- Exit WordPad
- Open a Document

- Print a Document
- Select Text
- Change Font Size
- Change Font Type
- Edit Text

- Move Text
- **Bold, Italic and Underline**
- **Change Alignment of Text**

You can enhance the appearance of your document by aligning text in different ways.

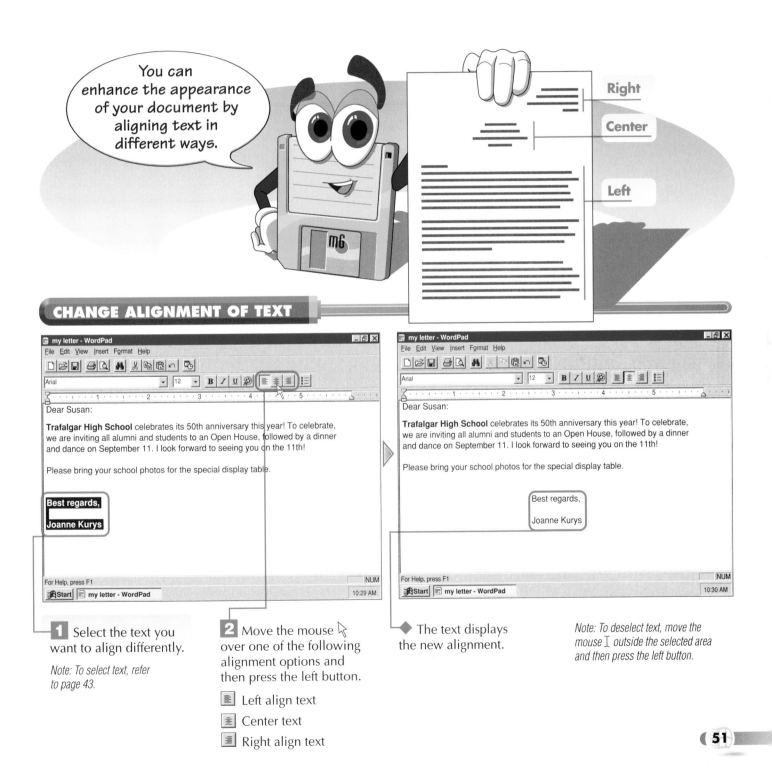

CHANGE ALIGNMENT OF TEXT

1 Select the text you want to align differently.

Note: To select text, refer to page 43.

2 Move the mouse over one of the following alignment options and then press the left button.

☰ Left align text

☰ Center text

☰ Right align text

◆ The text displays the new alignment.

Note: To deselect text, move the mouse I outside the selected area and then press the left button.

PAINT

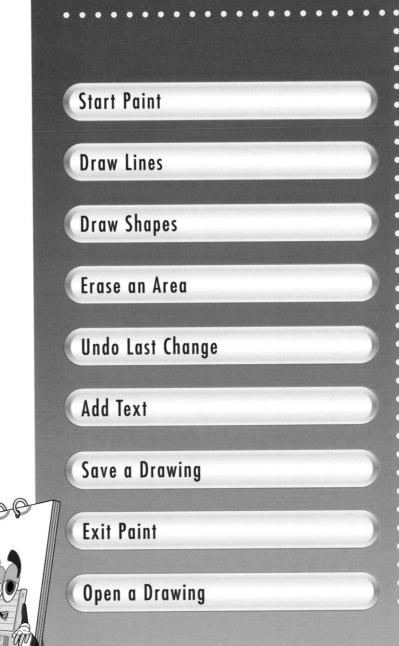

START PAINT

Paint lets you use your artistic abilities to draw pictures and maps on your computer.

START PAINT

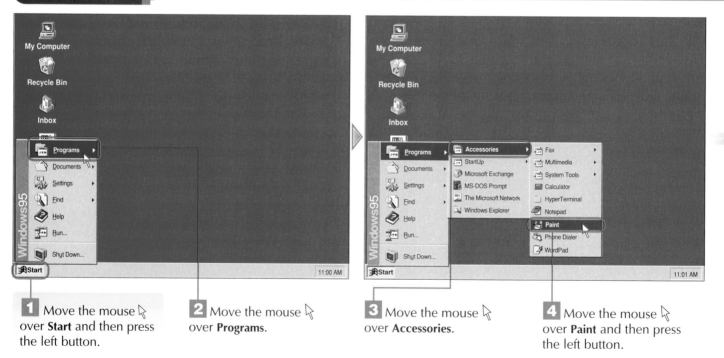

1 Move the mouse ⟨ over **Start** and then press the left button.

2 Move the mouse ⟨ over **Programs**.

3 Move the mouse ⟨ over **Accessories**.

4 Move the mouse ⟨ over **Paint** and then press the left button.

- **Start Paint**
- Draw Lines
- Draw Shapes
- Erase an Area
- Undo Last Change
- Add Text
- Save a Drawing
- Exit Paint
- Open a Drawing

Tip

You can place Paint drawings in other programs. For example, you can enhance the appearance of an invitation by adding a drawing you created.

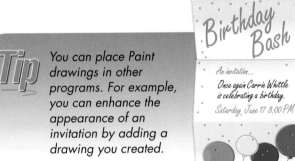

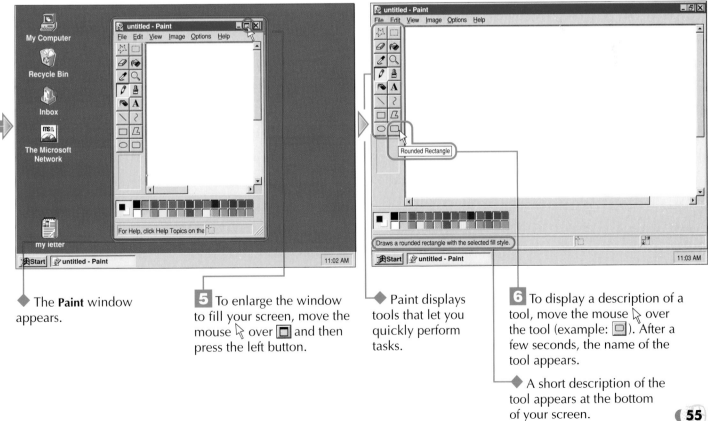

◆ The **Paint** window appears.

5 To enlarge the window to fill your screen, move the mouse ▷ over ⬜ and then press the left button.

◆ Paint displays tools that let you quickly perform tasks.

6 To display a description of a tool, move the mouse ▷ over the tool (example: ⬜). After a few seconds, the name of the tool appears.

◆ A short description of the tool appears at the bottom of your screen.

DRAW LINES

You can draw straight, wavy and curved lines in any color displayed at the bottom of your screen.

DRAW LINES

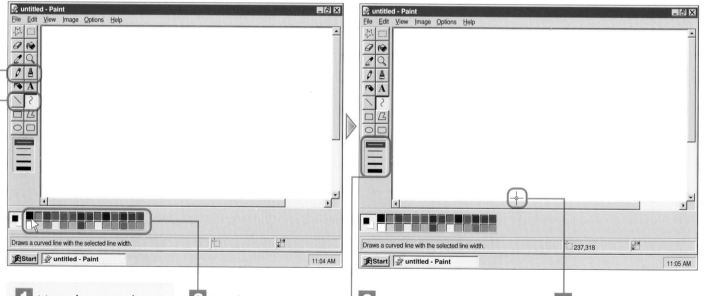

1 Move the mouse ⌖ over the line tool you want to use (example: ⌇) and then press the left button.

2 To select a color for the line, move the mouse ⌖ over the color (example: ■) and then press the left button.

3 To select a line thickness, move the mouse ⌖ over one of these options and then press the left button.

Note: The ⌇ tool does not provide any line thickness options. The ⌷ tool provides a different set of options.

4 Move the mouse ⌖ to where you want to begin drawing the line and ⌖ changes to ┼ or ⌇.

Paint lets you draw these types of lines.

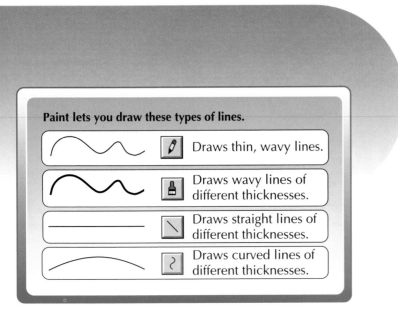

~~	✐	Draws thin, wavy lines.
~	▦	Draws wavy lines of different thicknesses.
───	⬉	Draws straight lines of different thicknesses.
⌢	⌇	Draws curved lines of different thicknesses.

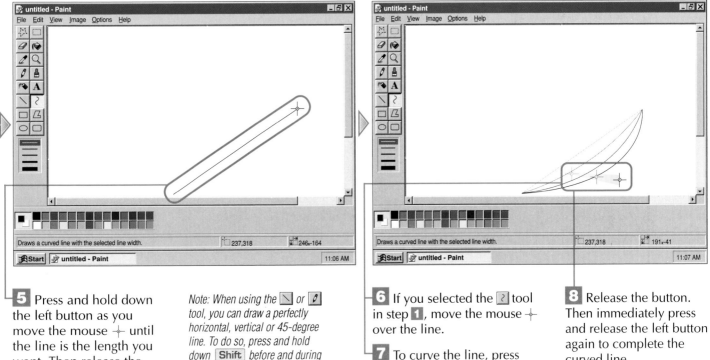

5 Press and hold down the left button as you move the mouse ✛ until the line is the length you want. Then release the button.

Note: When using the ⬉ or ✐ tool, you can draw a perfectly horizontal, vertical or 45-degree line. To do so, press and hold down **Shift** *before and during step* **5** .

6 If you selected the ⌇ tool in step **1**, move the mouse ✛ over the line.

7 To curve the line, press and hold down the left button. Then drag the line until it curves the way you want.

8 Release the button. Then immediately press and release the left button again to complete the curved line.

You should save your drawing to store it for future use. This lets you later review and make changes to the drawing.

SAVE A DRAWING

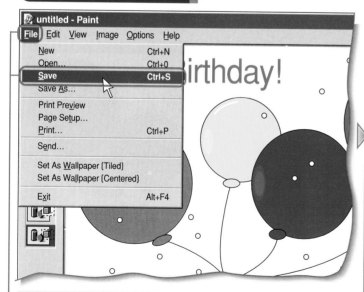

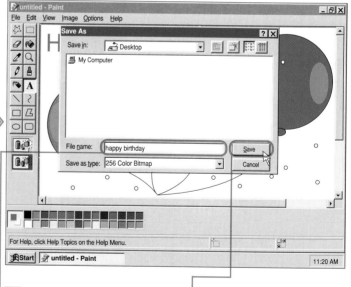

1 Move the mouse ☐ over **File** and then press the left button.

2 Move the mouse ☐ over **Save** and then press the left button.

◆ The **Save As** dialog box appears.

*Note: If you previously saved your drawing, the **Save As** dialog box will not appear, since you have already named the drawing.*

3 Type a name for your drawing.

*Note: You can use up to 255 characters to name your drawing. The name cannot contain the characters \ ? : * " < > or |.*

4 Move the mouse ☐ over **Save** and then press the left button.

- Start Paint
- Draw Lines
- Draw Shapes
- Erase an Area
- Undo Last Change
- Add Text
- **Save a Drawing**
- **Exit Paint**
- Open a Drawing

When you finish using Paint, you can exit the program.

EXIT PAINT

◆ Paint saves your drawing and displays the name at the top of your screen.

SAVE CHANGES

To avoid losing your work, you should save your drawing every 5 to 10 minutes.

◆ To save changes, repeat steps **1** and **2**.

1 Move the mouse ⬚ over **X** and then press the left button.

65

You can open a saved drawing and display it on your screen. This lets you view and make changes to the drawing.

◆ To start **Paint**, refer to page 54.

1 Move the mouse ↻ over **File** and then press the left button.

2 Move the mouse ↻ over **Open** and then press the left button.

◆ The **Open** dialog box appears.

3 Move the mouse ↻ over the name of the drawing you want to open and then press the left button.

Note: If you cannot find the drawing you want to open, refer to page 108 to find the drawing.

4 Move the mouse ↻ over **Open** and then press the left button.

IMPORTANT!

Paint only lets you work with one drawing at a time. If you are currently working with a drawing, save the drawing before opening another.

Note: For information on saving a drawing, refer to page 64.

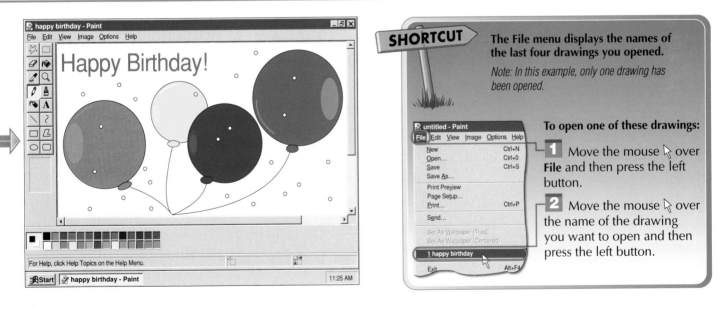

SHORTCUT

The File menu displays the names of the last four drawings you opened.

Note: In this example, only one drawing has been opened.

To open one of these drawings:

1 Move the mouse over **File** and then press the left button.

2 Move the mouse over the name of the drawing you want to open and then press the left button.

◆ Paint opens the drawing and displays it on your screen. You can now review and make changes to the drawing.

VIEW CONTENTS
OF COMPUTER

Storage Devices

View Contents of Computer

Change Size of Items

Move an Item

Arrange Items

Display File Information

Sort Items

HARD DRIVE (C:)

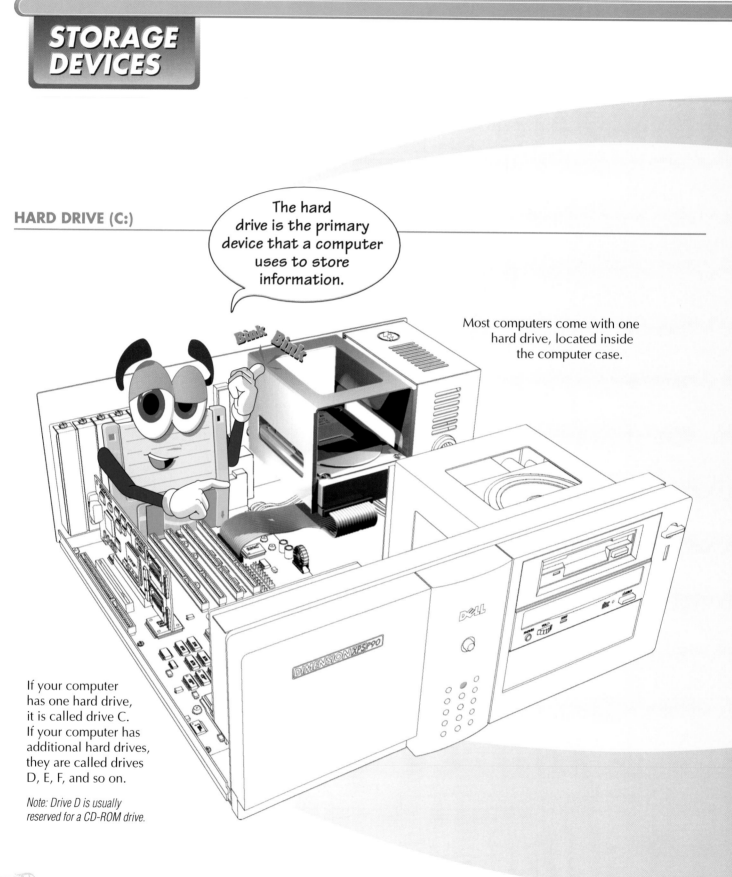

The hard drive is the primary device that a computer uses to store information.

Most computers come with one hard drive, located inside the computer case.

If your computer has one hard drive, it is called drive C. If your computer has additional hard drives, they are called drives D, E, F, and so on.

Note: Drive D is usually reserved for a CD-ROM drive.

FLOPPY DRIVE (A:)

A floppy drive stores and retrieves information on floppy disks (diskettes). If your computer has only one floppy drive, it is called drive A. If your computer has two floppy drives, the second drive is called drive B.

CD-ROM DRIVE (D:)

A CD-ROM drive is a device that reads information stored on compact discs. You cannot change information stored on a compact disc.

Note: Your computer may not have a CD-ROM drive.

VIEW CONTENTS OF COMPUTER

You can easily view the folders and files stored on your computer.

Like a filing cabinet, your computer uses folders to organize information.

VIEW CONTENTS OF YOUR COMPUTER

1 To view the contents of your computer, move the mouse ⊳ over **My Computer** and then quickly press the left button twice.

◆ The **My Computer** window opens.

◆ The taskbar displays the name of the opened window.

◆ These objects represent the drives on your computer.

2 To display the contents of a drive, move the mouse ⊳ over the drive (example: **C:**) and then quickly press the left button twice.

Note: If you want to view the contents of a floppy or CD-ROM drive, make sure you insert a floppy disk or CD-ROM disc before performing step **2**.

- Storage Devices
- **View Contents of Computer**
- Change Size of Items
- Move an Item

- Arrange Items
- Display File Information
- Sort Items

Tip

Folder

A folder stores related information. It can contain files and other folders.

File

A file is a named collection of information. The picture above the file name helps identify the file type.

Hard Disk (C:)
File Edit View Help

Exchange   Program Files   Windows

Command   Netlog

5 object(s)   774KB

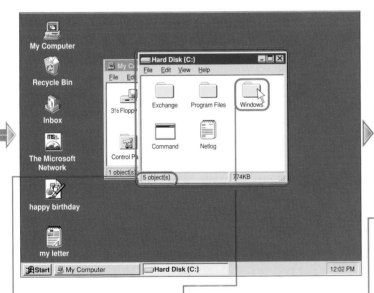

◆ A window appears, displaying the contents of the drive.

◆ This area tells you how many objects are in the window.

3 To display the contents of a folder, move the mouse over the folder (example: **Windows**) and then quickly press the left button twice.

◆ A new window appears, displaying the contents of the folder.

You can change the size of items displayed in a window. Enlarging items lets you view the items more clearly.

CHANGE SIZE OF ITEMS

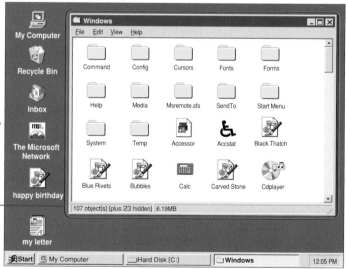

1 Move the mouse ▷ over **View** and then press the left button.

2 To enlarge the items in a window, move the mouse ▷ over **Large Icons** and then press the left button.

◆ The items change to a larger size.

*Note: To return to the smaller item size, repeat steps **1** and **2**, selecting **Small Icons** in step **2**.*

74

You can move an item to a new location in a window. This lets you rearrange items as you would rearrange objects on your desk.

MOVE AN ITEM

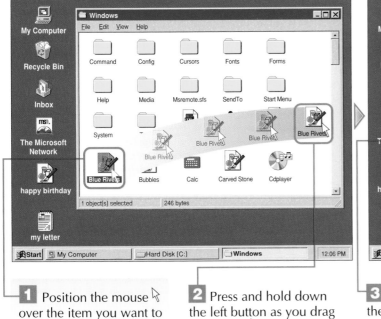
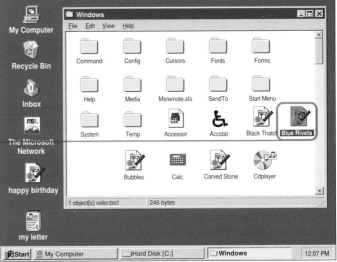

1 Position the mouse ⍗ over the item you want to move.

2 Press and hold down the left button as you drag the mouse ⍗ to where you want to place the item.

3 Release the button and the item moves to the new location.

*Note: If the **Auto Arrange** feature is on, other items will automatically adjust to make room for the item. For more information, refer to page 76.*

ARRANGE ITEMS

You can have Windows automatically arrange items to fit neatly in a window.

ARRANGE ITEMS

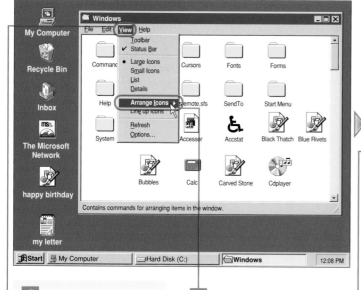

1 Move the mouse ⊳ over **View** and then press the left button.

2 Move the mouse ⊳ over **Arrange Icons**.

◆ If this area does not display a check mark (✔), the Auto Arrange feature is off.

3 To turn on the feature, move the mouse ⊳ over **Auto Arrange** and then press the left button.

Note: If the area displays a check mark (✔) and you want to leave the feature on, press **Alt** *on your keyboard to close the menu.*

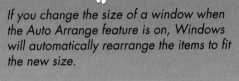

Tip

If you change the size of a window when the Auto Arrange feature is on, Windows will automatically rearrange the items to fit the new size.

Note: For information on changing the size of a window, refer to page 20.

◆ The items fit neatly in the window.

◆ To turn off the Auto Arrange feature, repeat steps **1** to **3**.

Note: You cannot move an item to a blank area in a window when the Auto Arrange feature is on.

Windows lets you display information about the files listed in a window.

DISPLAY FILE INFORMATION

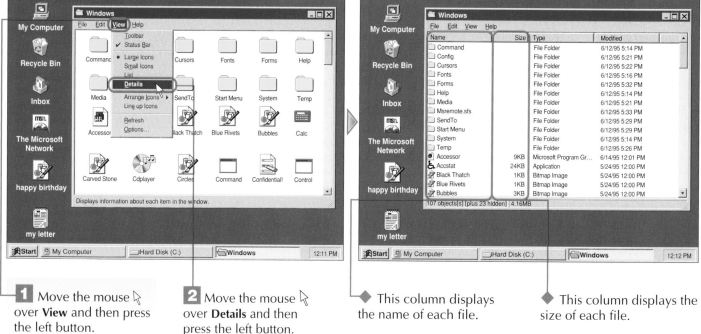

1 Move the mouse over **View** and then press the left button.

2 Move the mouse over **Details** and then press the left button.

◆ This column displays the name of each file.

◆ This column displays the size of each file.

- Storage Devices
- View Contents of Computer
- Change Size of Items
- Move an Item
- Arrange Items
- **Display File Information**
- Sort Items

The size of a file is measured in kilobytes (KB). A kilobyte is approximately 1,000 characters, or one page of double spaced text.

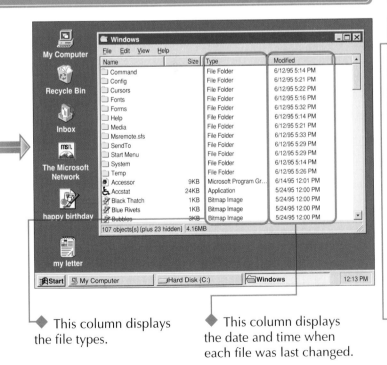

DISPLAY NAMES ONLY

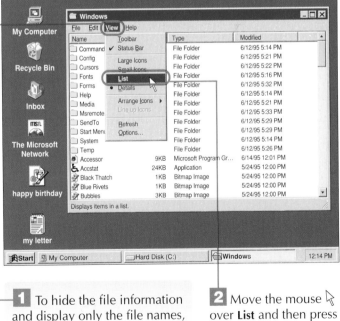

◆ This column displays the file types.

◆ This column displays the date and time when each file was last changed.

1 To hide the file information and display only the file names, move the mouse ▷ over **View** and then press the left button.

2 Move the mouse ▷ over **List** and then press the left button.

SORT ITEMS

You can sort the items displayed in a window. This can help you find files and folders more easily.

NAME SORT ITEMS

SIZE SORT ITEMS

TYPE SORT ITEMS

DATE SORT ITEMS

SORT BY NAME

1 To sort the item names from A to Z, move the mouse � over **Name** and then press the left button.

*Note: If the **Name** button is not displayed, perform steps **1** and **2** on page 78.*

◆ The items in the window are sorted.

*Note: To sort the item names from Z to A, repeat step **1**.*

SORT BY SIZE

1 To sort the items from smallest to largest, move the mouse � over **Size** and then press the left button.

*Note: If the **Size** button is not displayed, perform steps **1** and **2** on page 78.*

◆ The items in the window are sorted.

*Note: To sort the items from largest to smallest, repeat step **1**.*

- Storage Devices
- View Contents of Computer
- Change Size of Items
- Move an Item
- Arrange Items
- Display File Information
- Sort Items

No matter how you sort items, Windows always lists the folders separately from the files.

SORT BY TYPE

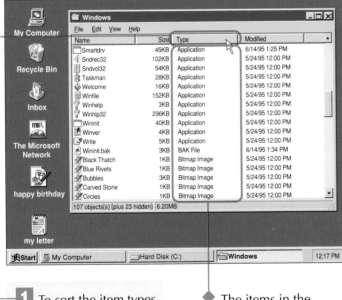

1 To sort the item types from A to Z, move the mouse ⌖ over **Type** and then press the left button.

*Note: If the **Type** button is not displayed, perform steps **1** and **2** on page 78.*

◆ The items in the window are sorted.

*Note: To sort the item types from Z to A, repeat step **1**.*

SORT BY DATE

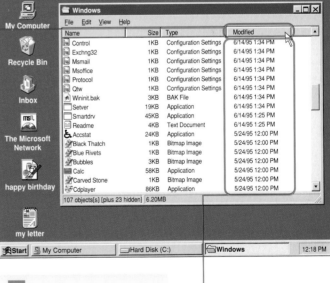

1 To sort the items from newest to oldest, move the mouse ⌖ over **Modified** and then press the left button.

*Note: If the **Modified** button is not displayed, perform steps **1** and **2** on page 78.*

◆ The items in the window are sorted.

*Note: To sort the items from oldest to newest, repeat step **1**.*

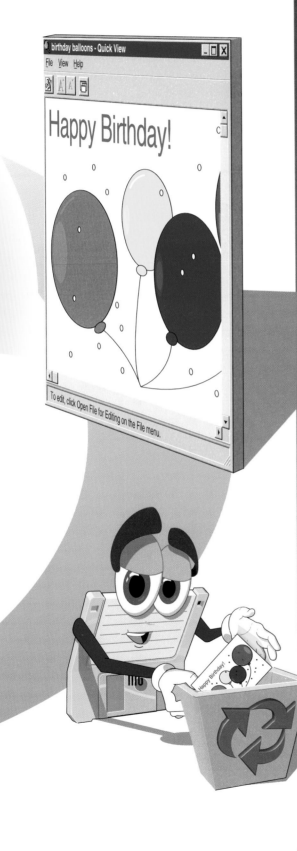

WORK WITH FILES AND FOLDERS

Select Files

Create a New Folder

Move a File to a Folder

Copy a File to a Floppy Disk

Rename a File

Open a File

Preview a File

Print a File

View Files Sent to Printer

Pause the Printer

Cancel Printing

Delete a File

Restore a Deleted File

Empty the Recycle Bin

Find a File

Add a Shortcut to the Desktop

Before working with files, you must first select the files you want to work with. Selected files appear highlighted on your screen.

SELECT A FILE

1 Move the mouse ⓚ over the file you want to select and then press the left button.

◆ The file is highlighted.

Note: To deselect files, move the mouse ⓚ over a blank area in the window and then press the left button.

◆ This area displays the number of files you selected.

◆ This area displays the total size of the files you selected.

Note: One byte equals one character. One kilobyte (KB) equals approximately one page of double spaced text.

- **Select Files**
- Create a New Folder
- Move a File to a Folder
- Copy a File to a Floppy Disk
- Rename a File
- Open a File

- Preview a File
- Print a File
- View Files Sent to Printer
- Pause the Printer
- Cancel Printing
- Delete a File

- Restore a Deleted File
- Empty the Recycle Bin
- Find a File
- Add a Shortcut to the Desktop

Tip

SELECT FOLDERS

You can use the methods described below to select folders.

SELECT A GROUP OF FILES

1 Move the mouse ⌖ over the first file you want to select and then press the left button.

2 Press and hold down `Shift` on your keyboard.

3 Still holding down `Shift`, move the mouse ⌖ over the last file you want to select and then press the left button.

SELECT ANY FILES

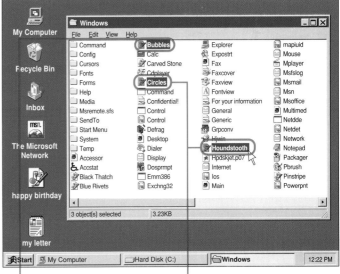

1 Move the mouse ⌖ over a file you want to select and then press the left button.

2 Press and hold down `Ctrl` on your keyboard.

3 Still holding down `Ctrl`, repeat step **1** for each file you want to select.

CREATE A NEW FOLDER

You can create a new folder to better organize the information stored on your computer. Creating a folder is like placing a new folder in a filing cabinet.

A folder is also called a directory.

CREATE A NEW FOLDER

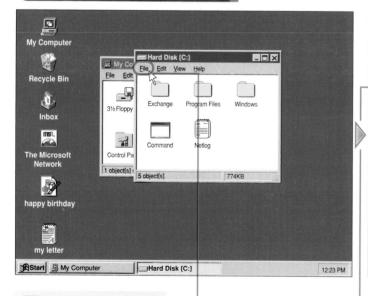

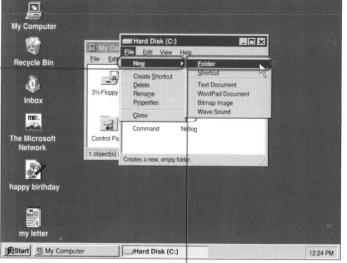

1 Display the contents of the drive or folder where you want to place the new folder.

Note: For information, refer to page 72.

2 To deselect any selected files, move the mouse ⟶ over a blank area in the window and then press the left button.

3 Move the mouse ⟶ over **File** and then press the left button.

4 Move the mouse ⟶ over **New**.

5 Move the mouse ⟶ over **Folder** and then press the left button.

- Select Files
- **Create a New Folder**
- Move a File to a Folder
- Copy a File to a Floppy Disk
- Rename a File
- Open a File

- Preview a File
- Print a File
- View Files Sent to Printer
- Pause the Printer
- Cancel Printing
- Delete a File

- Restore a Deleted File
- Empty the Recycle Bin
- Find a File
- Add a Shortcut to the Desktop

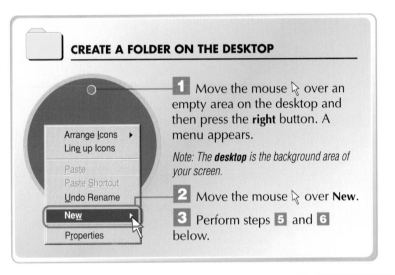

CREATE A FOLDER ON THE DESKTOP

1 Move the mouse ⍔ over an empty area on the desktop and then press the **right** button. A menu appears.

*Note: The **desktop** is the background area of your screen.*

2 Move the mouse ⍔ over **New**.

3 Perform steps **5** and **6** below.

Arrange Icons ▸
Line up Icons

Paste
Paste Shortcut
Undo Rename

New ▸

Properties

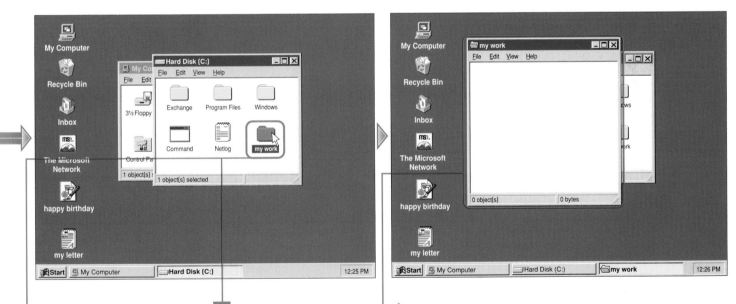

◆ The new folder appears, displaying a temporary name (New Folder).

6 Type a name for the new folder (example: **my work**) and then press Enter .

7 To display the contents of the new folder, move the mouse ⍔ over the folder and then quickly press the left button twice.

◆ The contents of the folder appear.

Note: To close a window, move the mouse ⍔ over X and then press the left button.

MOVE A FILE TO A FOLDER

You can reorganize the files stored on your computer by placing them in different folders.

Moving files is similar to rearranging documents in a filing cabinet to make them easier to find.

MOVE A FILE TO A FOLDER

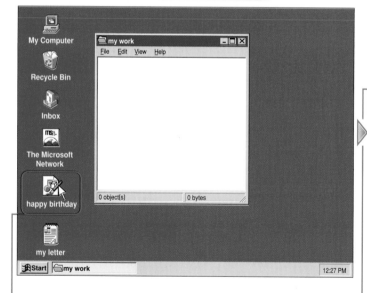

1 Position the mouse ▷ over the file you want to move.

◆ To move more than one file, select all the files you want to move. Then position the mouse ▷ over one of the files.

Note: To select multiple files, refer to page 85.

2 Press and hold down the left button as you drag the mouse ▷ to where you want to place the file.

- Select Files
- Create a New Folder
- **Move a File to a Folder**
- Copy a File to a Floppy Disk
- Rename a File
- Open a File

- Preview a File
- Print a File
- View Files Sent to Printer
- Pause the Printer
- Cancel Printing
- Delete a File

- Restore a Deleted File
- Empty the Recycle Bin
- Find a File
- Add a Shortcut to the Desktop

COPY A FILE TO A FOLDER

You can make an exact copy of a file and then place the copy in a new folder. This lets you store the file in two locations.

To copy a file, perform steps **1** to **3** below, except press and hold down `Ctrl` on your keyboard before and during step **3**.

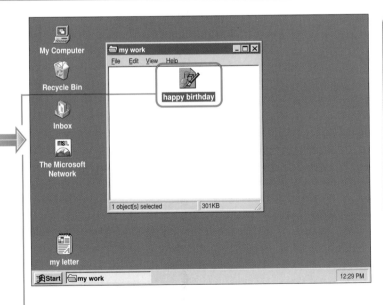

3 Release the button and the file moves to the new location.

MOVE A FOLDER

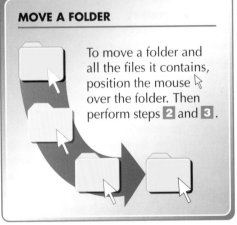

To move a folder and all the files it contains, position the mouse over the folder. Then perform steps **2** and **3**.

COPY A FILE TO A FLOPPY DISK

You can make an exact copy of a file and then place the copy on a floppy disk. This is useful if you want to give a copy of a file to a colleague.

COPY A FILE TO A FLOPPY DISK

1 Insert a floppy disk into a drive.

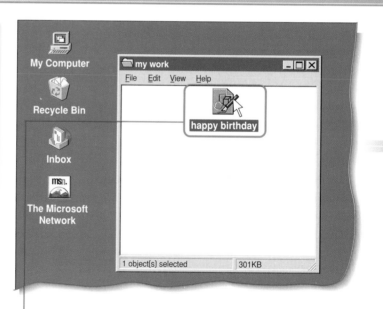

2 To select the file you want to copy, move the mouse over the file and then press the left button.

◆ To copy more than one file, select all the files you want to copy.

Note: To select multiple files, refer to page 85.

- Select Files
- Create a New Folder
- Move a File to a Folder
- **Copy a File to a Floppy Disk**
- Rename a File
- Open a File

- Preview a File
- Print a File
- View Files Sent to Printer
- Pause the Printer
- Cancel Printing
- Delete a File

- Restore a Deleted File
- Empty the Recycle Bin
- Find a File
- Add a Shortcut to the Desktop

Tip

Windows provides a backup program that helps you copy all your important files to floppy disks. This provides you with extra copies in case the original files are lost or damaged.

Note: To back up files, refer to the Back Up Your Files chapter, starting on page 192.

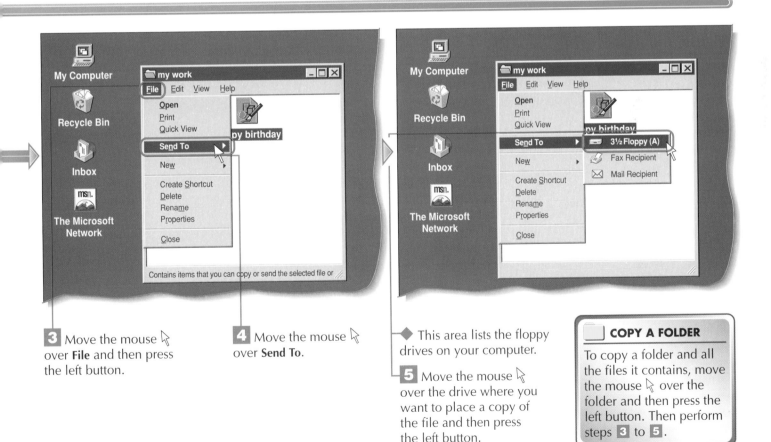

3 Move the mouse ⌖ over **File** and then press the left button.

4 Move the mouse ⌖ over **Send To**.

◆ This area lists the floppy drives on your computer.

5 Move the mouse ⌖ over the drive where you want to place a copy of the file and then press the left button.

COPY A FOLDER

To copy a folder and all the files it contains, move the mouse ⌖ over the folder and then press the left button. Then perform steps **3** to **5**.

RENAME A FILE

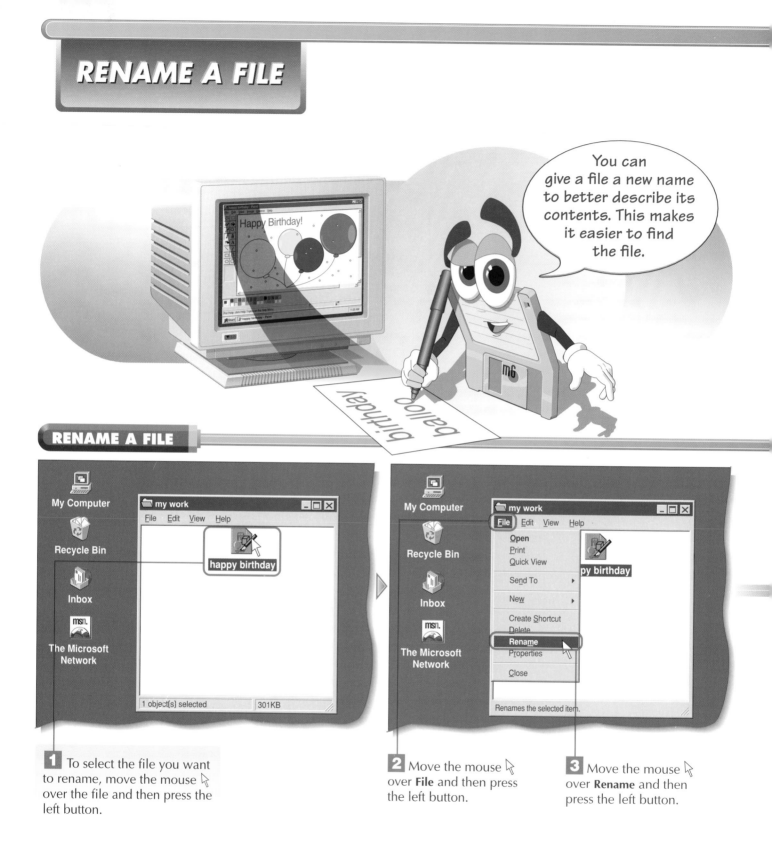

You can give a file a new name to better describe its contents. This makes it easier to find the file.

RENAME A FILE

1 To select the file you want to rename, move the mouse 🔓 over the file and then press the left button.

2 Move the mouse 🔓 over **File** and then press the left button.

3 Move the mouse 🔓 over **Rename** and then press the left button.

- Select Files
- Create a New Folder
- Move a File to a Folder
- Copy a File to a Floppy Disk
- **Rename a File**
- Open a File

- Preview a File
- Print a File
- View Files Sent to Printer
- Pause the Printer
- Cancel Printing
- Delete a File

- Restore a Deleted File
- Empty the Recycle Bin
- Find a File
- Add a Shortcut to the Desktop

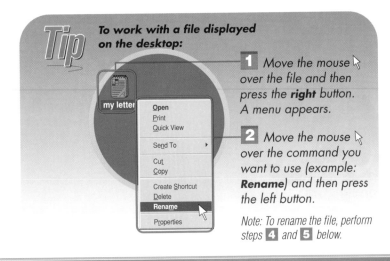

Tip

To work with a file displayed on the desktop:

1 Move the mouse over the file and then press the **right** button. A menu appears.

2 Move the mouse over the command you want to use (example: **Rename**) and then press the left button.

Note: To rename the file, perform steps **4** *and* **5** *below.*

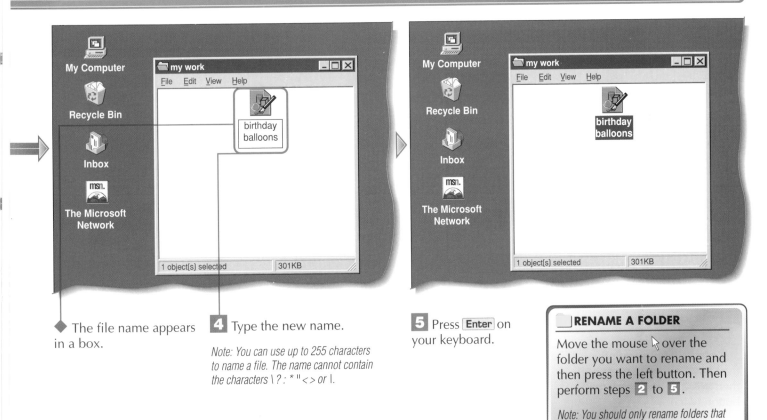

◆ The file name appears in a box.

4 Type the new name.

*Note: You can use up to 255 characters to name a file. The name cannot contain the characters \ ? : * " < > or |.*

5 Press **Enter** on your keyboard.

RENAME A FOLDER

Move the mouse over the folder you want to rename and then press the left button. Then perform steps **2** to **5**.

Note: You should only rename folders that you have created.

You can produce a paper copy of a file stored on your computer. Before printing, make sure your printer is on and contains paper.

PRINT A FILE

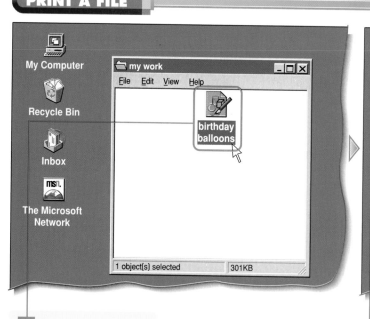

1 To select the file you want to print, move the mouse ⤢ over the file and then press the left button.

◆ To print more than one file, select the files.

Note: To select multiple files, refer to page 85.

2 Move the mouse ⤢ over **File** and then press the left button.

3 Move the mouse ⤢ over **Print** and then press the left button.

- Select Files
- Create a New Folder
- Move a File to a Folder
- Copy a File to a Floppy Disk
- Rename a File
- Open a File

- Preview a File
- **Print a File**
- **View Files Sent to Printer**
- Pause the Printer
- Cancel Printing
- Delete a File

- Restore a Deleted File
- Empty the Recycle Bin
- Find a File
- Add a Shortcut to the Desktop

> You can view information about the files you sent to the printer.

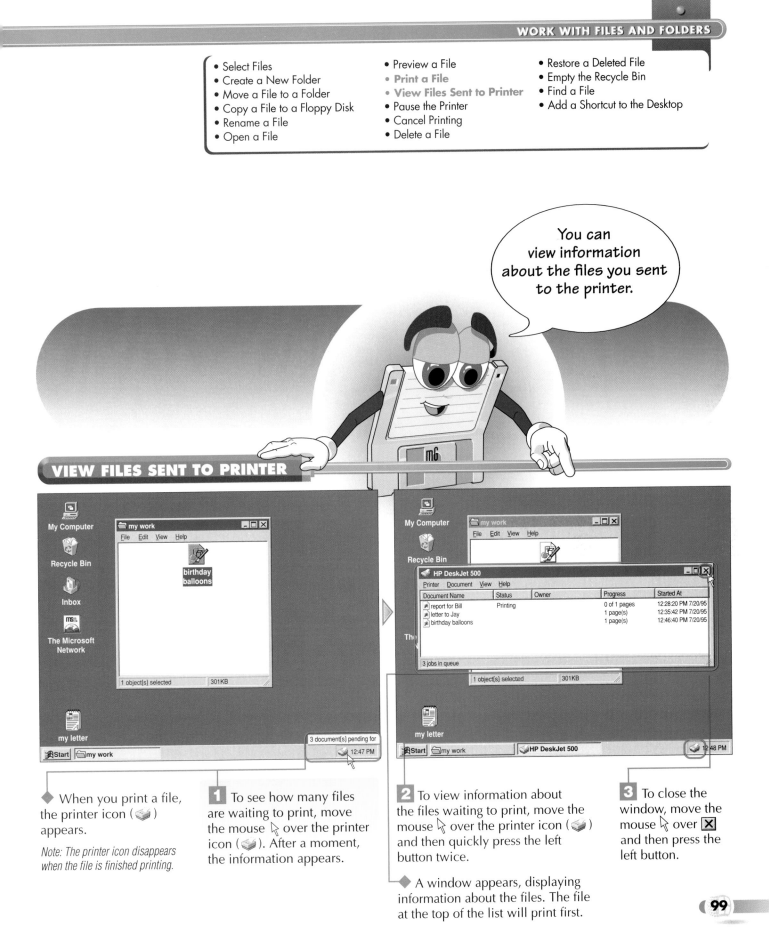

VIEW FILES SENT TO PRINTER

◆ When you print a file, the printer icon (🖨) appears.

Note: The printer icon disappears when the file is finished printing.

1 To see how many files are waiting to print, move the mouse ▷ over the printer icon (🖨). After a moment, the information appears.

2 To view information about the files waiting to print, move the mouse ▷ over the printer icon (🖨) and then quickly press the left button twice.

◆ A window appears, displaying information about the files. The file at the top of the list will print first.

3 To close the window, move the mouse ▷ over ✕ and then press the left button.

99

You can pause your printer and then resume printing at any time. This is useful when you want to change the type of paper in the printer.

PAUSE THE PRINTER

1 Move the mouse ⊾ over the printer icon (🖨) and then quickly press the left button twice.

◆ A window appears, displaying information about the files waiting to print.

2 Move the mouse ⊾ over **Printer** and then press the left button.

3 Move the mouse ⊾ over **Pause Printing** and then press the left button.

◆ The word **Paused** appears at the top of the window.

4 To restart the printer, repeat steps **2** and **3**.

5 To close the window, move the mouse ⊾ over **X** and then press the left button.

- Select Files
- Create a New Folder
- Move a File to a Folder
- Copy a File to a Floppy Disk
- Rename a File
- Open a File

- Preview a File
- Print a File
- View Files Sent to Printer
- **Pause the Printer**
- **Cancel Printing**
- Delete a File

- Restore a Deleted File
- Empty the Recycle Bin
- Find a File
- Add a Shortcut to the Desktop

You can cancel the printing of a file if you forgot to make last minute changes.

CANCEL PRINTING

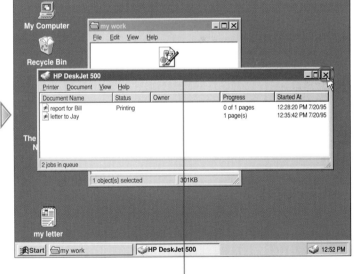

1 Move the mouse ⏳ over the printer icon (🖨️) and then quickly press the left button twice.

◆ A window appears, displaying information about the files waiting to print.

2 Move the mouse ⏳ over the file you no longer want to print and then press the left button.

3 Press **Delete** on your keyboard and the file disappears from the list.

4 To close the window, move the mouse ⏳ over **X** and then press the left button.

You can delete a file that you no longer need.

DELETE A FILE

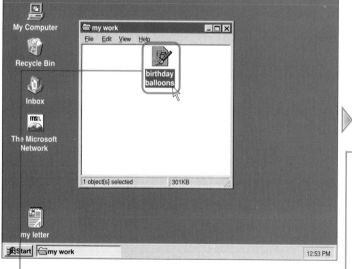

1 To select the file you want to delete, move the mouse ⇩ over the file and then press the left button.

◆ To delete more than one file, select the files.

Note: To select multiple files, refer to page 85.

2 Press Delete on your keyboard and the **Confirm File Delete** dialog box appears.

3 To delete the file, move the mouse ⇩ over **Yes** and then press the left button.

- Select Files
- Create a New Folder
- Move a File to a Folder
- Copy a File to a Floppy Disk
- Rename a File
- Open a File

- Preview a File
- Print a File
- View Files Sent to Printer
- Pause the Printer
- Cancel Printing
- **Delete a File**

- Restore a Deleted File
- Empty the Recycle Bin
- Find a File
- Add a Shortcut to the Desktop

Tip

You can restore files you have deleted.

Note: For more information, refer to page 104.

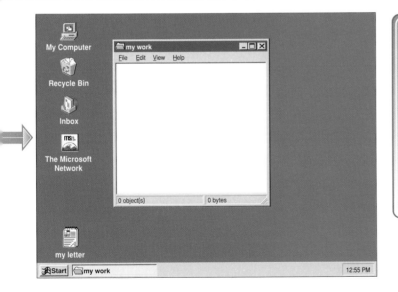

◆ The file disappears.

Note: To close a window, refer to page 27.

DELETE A FOLDER

You can delete a folder and all the files it contains.

1 To select the folder you want to delete, move the mouse ➢ over the folder and then press the left button.

2 Perform steps **2** and **3**.

The Recycle Bin stores all the files you have deleted. You can easily restore any of these files.

RESTORE A DELETED FILE

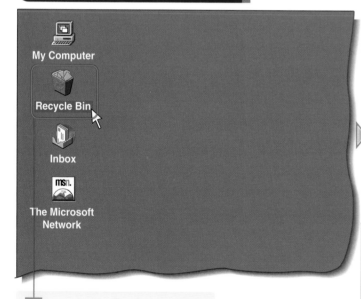

1 To display all the files you have deleted, move the mouse Ⓚ over **Recycle Bin** and then quickly press the left button twice.

◆ The **Recycle Bin** window appears, listing all the files you have deleted.

2 To select the file you want to restore, move the mouse Ⓚ over the file and then press the left button.

◆ To restore more than one file, select the files.

Note: To select multiple files, refer to page 85.

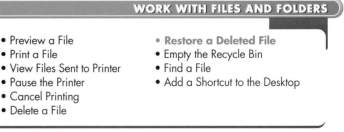
- Select Files
- Create a New Folder
- Move a File to a Folder
- Copy a File to a Floppy Disk
- Rename a File
- Open a File

- Preview a File
- Print a File
- View Files Sent to Printer
- Pause the Printer
- Cancel Printing
- Delete a File

- **Restore a Deleted File**
- Empty the Recycle Bin
- Find a File
- Add a Shortcut to the Desktop

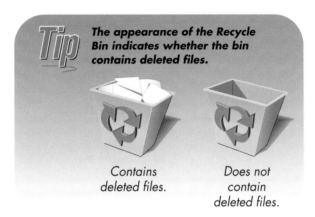

Tip

The appearance of the Recycle Bin indicates whether the bin contains deleted files.

Contains deleted files.

Does not contain deleted files.

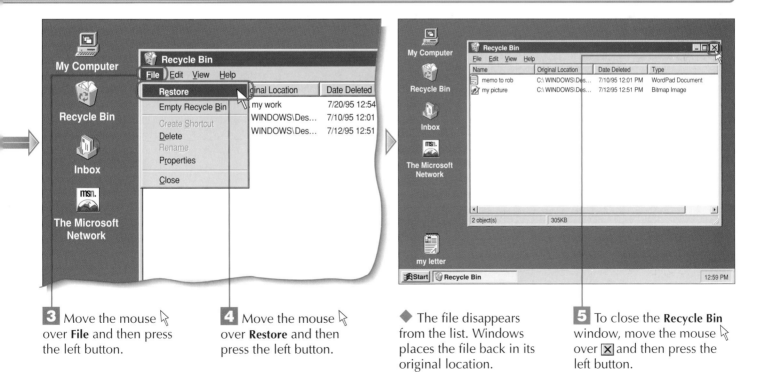

3 Move the mouse ⟋ over **File** and then press the left button.

4 Move the mouse ⟋ over **Restore** and then press the left button.

◆ The file disappears from the list. Windows places the file back in its original location.

5 To close the **Recycle Bin** window, move the mouse ⟋ over ☒ and then press the left button.

EMPTY THE RECYCLE BIN

You can create more space on your computer by permanently removing all the files from the Recycle Bin.

EMPTY THE RECYCLE BIN

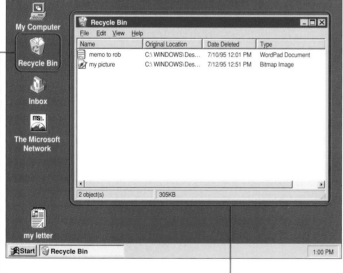

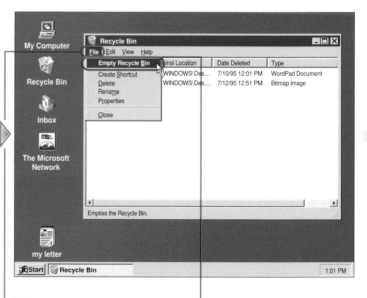

1 To display all the files you have deleted, move the mouse ⊳ over **Recycle Bin** and then quickly press the left button twice.

◆ The **Recycle Bin** window appears, listing all the files you have deleted.

2 Move the mouse ⊳ over **File** and then press the left button.

3 Move the mouse ⊳ over **Empty Recycle Bin** and then press the left button.

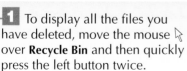

- Select Files
- Create a New Folder
- Move a File to a Folder
- Copy a File to a Floppy Disk
- Rename a File
- Open a File

- Preview a File
- Print a File
- View Files Sent to Printer
- Pause the Printer
- Cancel Printing
- Delete a File

- Restore a Deleted File
- **Empty the Recycle Bin**
- Find a File
- Add a Shortcut to the Desktop

IMPORTANT!

Before emptying the Recycle Bin, make sure it does not contain files you may need in the future.

◆ This dialog box appears.

4 To permanently delete all the files, move the mouse over **Yes** and then press the left button.

◆ All the files are deleted.

5 To close the **Recycle Bin** window, move the mouse over ☒ and then press the left button.

FIND A FILE

If you cannot remember the name or location of a file you want to work with, you can have Windows search for the file.

FIND A FILE

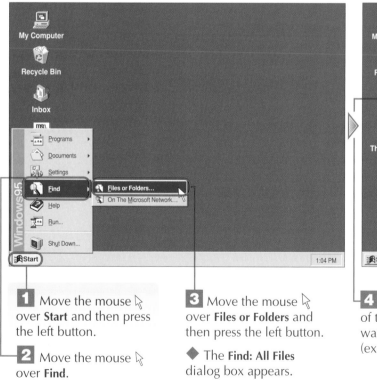

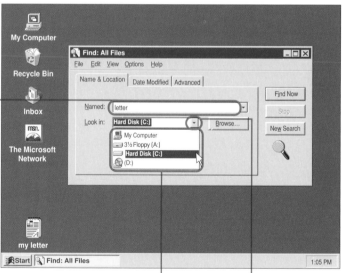

1 Move the mouse ⌖ over **Start** and then press the left button.

2 Move the mouse ⌖ over **Find**.

3 Move the mouse ⌖ over **Files or Folders** and then press the left button.

◆ The **Find: All Files** dialog box appears.

4 If you know all or part of the name of the file you want to find, type the name (example: **letter**).

5 To specify where you want Windows to search for the file, move the mouse ⌖ over ▾ in the **Look in:** box and then press the left button.

6 Move the mouse ⌖ over the location you want to search and then press the left button.

- Select Files
- Create a New Folder
- Move a File to a Folder
- Copy a File to a Floppy Disk
- Rename a File
- Open a File

- Preview a File
- Print a File
- View Files Sent to Printer
- Pause the Printer
- Cancel Printing
- Delete a File

- Restore a Deleted File
- Empty the Recycle Bin
- **Find a File**
- Add a Shortcut to the Desktop

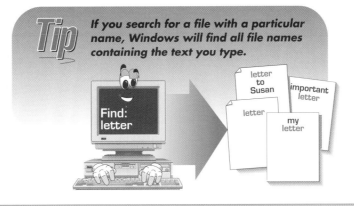

Tip

If you search for a file with a particular name, Windows will find all file names containing the text you type.

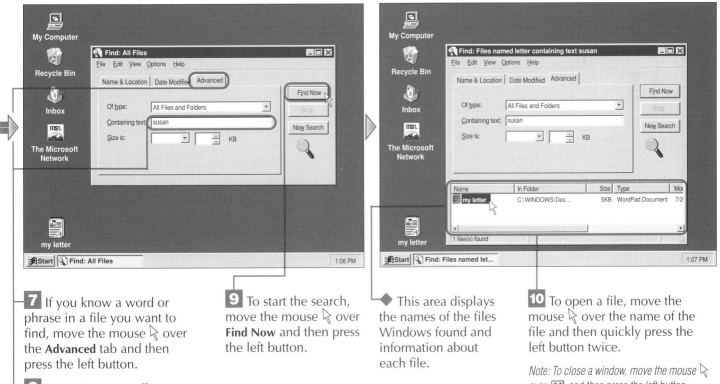

7 If you know a word or phrase in a file you want to find, move the mouse ⮕ over the **Advanced** tab and then press the left button.

8 Move the mouse I over the box beside **Containing text:** and then press the left button. Type the word or phrase (example: **susan**).

9 To start the search, move the mouse ⮕ over **Find Now** and then press the left button.

◆ This area displays the names of the files Windows found and information about each file.

10 To open a file, move the mouse ⮕ over the name of the file and then quickly press the left button twice.

Note: To close a window, move the mouse ⮕ over ✕ and then press the left button.

109

ADD A SHORTCUT TO THE DESKTOP

You can add a shortcut to the desktop to provide a quick way of opening a file you use regularly.

ADD A SHORTCUT TO THE DESKTOP

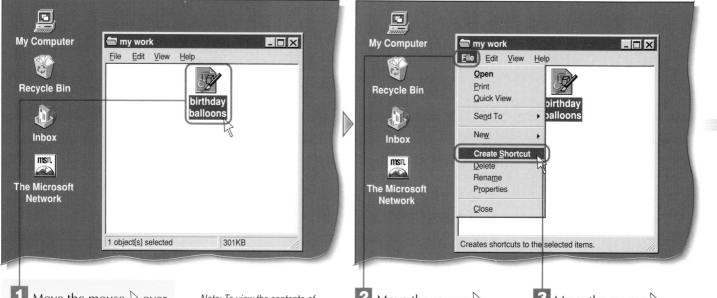

1 Move the mouse ⇧ over the file you want to create a shortcut to and then press the left button.

Note: To view the contents of your computer and display the file you want to create a shortcut to, refer to page 72.

2 Move the mouse ⇧ over **File** and then press the left button.

3 Move the mouse ⇧ over **Create Shortcut** and then press the left button.

- Select Files
- Create a New Folder
- Move a File to a Folder
- Copy a File to a Floppy Disk
- Rename a File
- Open a File

- Preview a File
- Print a File
- View Files Sent to Printer
- Pause the Printer
- Cancel Printing
- Delete a File

- Restore a Deleted File
- Empty the Recycle Bin
- Find a File
- **Add a Shortcut to the Desktop**

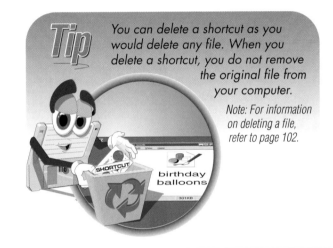

Tip

You can delete a shortcut as you would delete any file. When you delete a shortcut, you do not remove the original file from your computer.

Note: For information on deleting a file, refer to page 102.

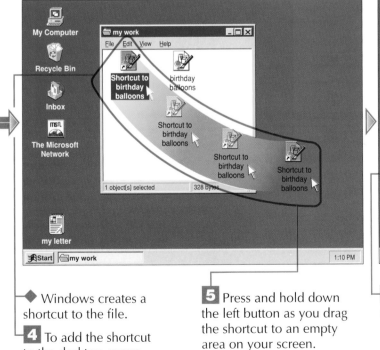

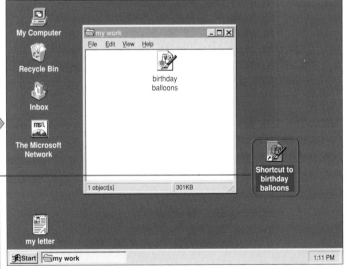

◆ Windows creates a shortcut to the file.

4 To add the shortcut to the desktop, move the mouse ⌖ over the shortcut.

5 Press and hold down the left button as you drag the shortcut to an empty area on your screen.

6 Release the button and the shortcut appears on the desktop.

Note: To open the file and display its contents on your screen, refer to page 94.

USING WINDOWS EXPLORER

Start Windows Explorer

Display or Hide Folders

Create a New Folder

Move a File to Another Folder

Delete a File

START WINDOWS EXPLORER

Like a map, Windows Explorer shows the location of every folder and file on your computer.

START WINDOWS EXPLORER

1 Move the mouse over **Start** and then press the left button.

2 Move the mouse over **Programs**.

3 Move the mouse over **Windows Explorer** and then press the left button.

◆ The **Exploring** window appears.

4 To enlarge the window to fill your screen, move the mouse over □ and then press the left button.

- **Start Windows Explorer**
- Display or Hide Folders
- Create a New Folder
- Move a File to Another Folder
- Delete a File

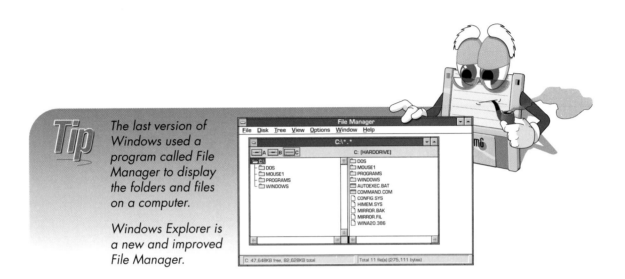

The last version of Windows used a program called File Manager to display the folders and files on a computer.

Windows Explorer is a new and improved File Manager.

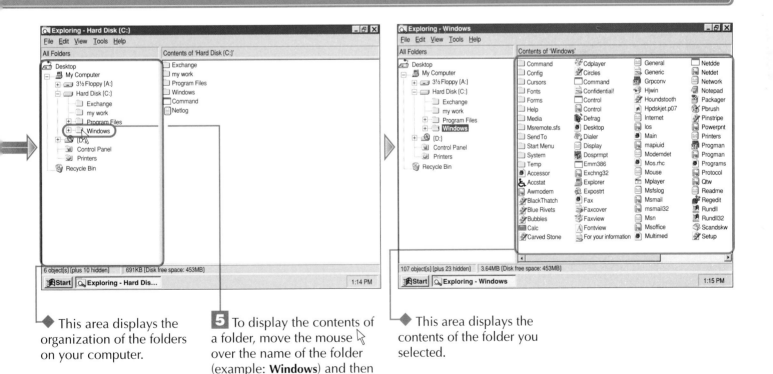

◆ This area displays the organization of the folders on your computer.

5 To display the contents of a folder, move the mouse over the name of the folder (example: **Windows**) and then press the left button.

◆ This area displays the contents of the folder you selected.

DISPLAY OR HIDE FOLDERS

A folder may contain other folders. You can easily display or hide these folders at any time.

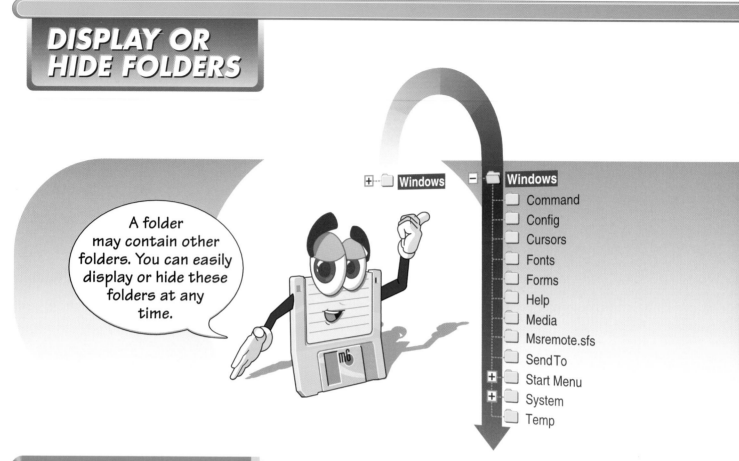

+ 🗀 Windows

− 📂 **Windows**
- 🗀 Command
- 🗀 Config
- 🗀 Cursors
- 🗀 Fonts
- 🗀 Forms
- 🗀 Help
- 🗀 Media
- 🗀 Msremote.sfs
- 🗀 SendTo
- + 🗀 Start Menu
- + 🗀 System
- 🗀 Temp

DISPLAY HIDDEN FOLDERS

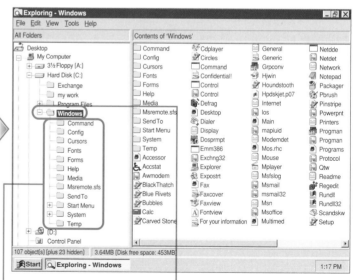

You display folders to view more of the contents of your computer.

1 To display the hidden folders within a folder, move the mouse ⍐ over the plus sign (⊞) beside the folder and then press the left button.

◆ The hidden folders appear.

◆ The plus sign (⊞) beside the folder changes to a minus sign (⊟). This indicates that all the folders within the folder are now displayed.

116

- Start Windows Explorer
- **Display or Hide Folders**
- Create a New Folder
- Move a File to Another Folder
- Delete a File

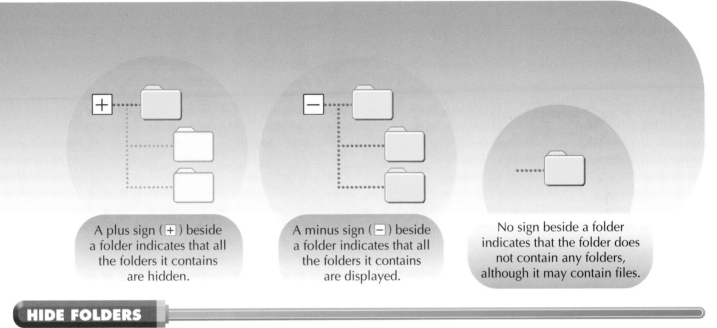

A plus sign (⊞) beside a folder indicates that all the folders it contains are hidden.

A minus sign (⊟) beside a folder indicates that all the folders it contains are displayed.

No sign beside a folder indicates that the folder does not contain any folders, although it may contain files.

HIDE FOLDERS

You hide folders to reduce the amount of information on your screen.

1 To hide the folders within a folder, move the mouse ☓ over the minus sign (⊟) beside the folder and then press the left button.

◆ The folders are hidden.

◆ The minus sign (⊟) beside the folder changes to a plus sign (⊞). This indicates that all the folders within the folder are now hidden.

CREATE A NEW FOLDER

You can create a new folder in Windows Explorer to improve the organization of your information. Creating a folder is like placing a new folder in a filing cabinet.

A folder is also called a directory.

CREATE A NEW FOLDER

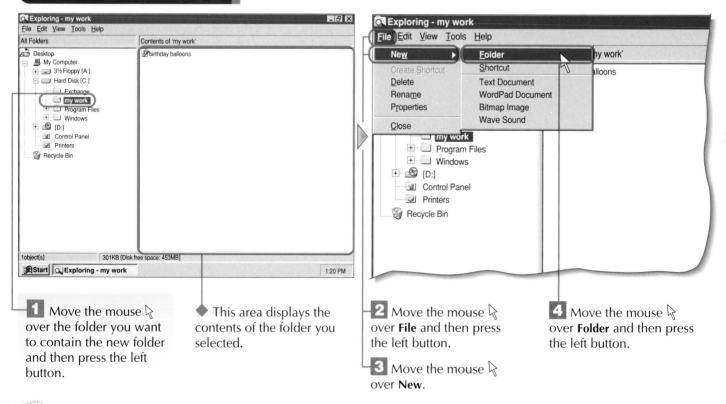

1 Move the mouse ⟍ over the folder you want to contain the new folder and then press the left button.

◆ This area displays the contents of the folder you selected.

2 Move the mouse ⟍ over **File** and then press the left button.

3 Move the mouse ⟍ over **New**.

4 Move the mouse ⟍ over **Folder** and then press the left button.

- Start Windows Explorer
- Display or Hide Folders
- **Create a New Folder**
- Move a File to Another Folder
- Delete a File

Tip

After creating a new folder, you can move files into the folder. This lets you keep related files in one location so they are easy to find.

Note: To move a file, refer to page 120.

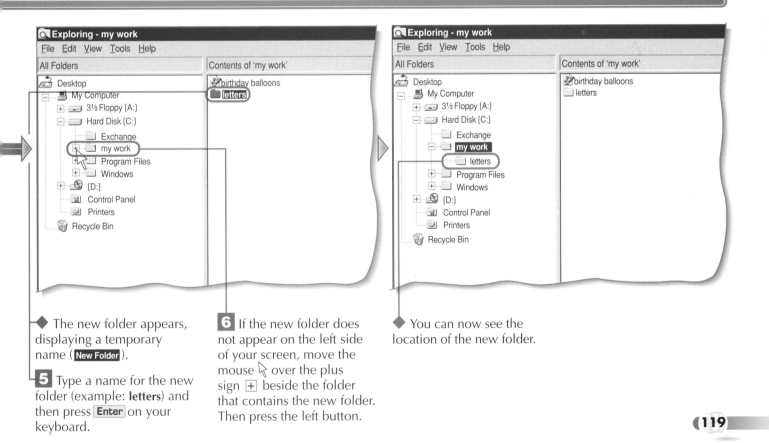

◆ The new folder appears, displaying a temporary name (New Folder).

5 Type a name for the new folder (example: **letters**) and then press **Enter** on your keyboard.

6 If the new folder does not appear on the left side of your screen, move the mouse ↖ over the plus sign ⊞ beside the folder that contains the new folder. Then press the left button.

◆ You can now see the location of the new folder.

MOVE A FILE TO ANOTHER FOLDER

In Windows Explorer, you can reorganize your files by placing them in other folders.

Moving files is similar to rearranging documents in a filing cabinet to make them easier to find.

MOVE A FILE TO ANOTHER FOLDER

1 Move the mouse ↖ over the item that contains the file you want to move and then press the left button.

◆ This area displays the contents of the item you selected.

2 Position the mouse ↖ over the file you want to move.

◆ To move more than one file, select all the files you want to move. Then position the mouse ↖ over one of the files.

Note: To select multiple files, refer to page 85.

- Start Windows Explorer
- Display or Hide Folders
- Create a New Folder
- **Move a File to Another Folder**
- Delete a File

COPY A FILE TO ANOTHER FOLDER

You can make an exact copy of a file and then place the copy in a new folder. This lets you store the file in two locations.

◆ To copy a file, perform steps **1** to **3** below, except press and hold down `Ctrl` on your keyboard during step **3**.

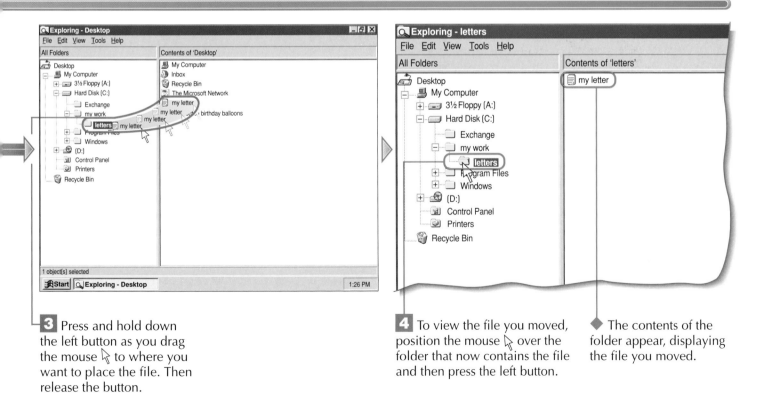

3 Press and hold down the left button as you drag the mouse ⟡ to where you want to place the file. Then release the button.

4 To view the file you moved, position the mouse ⟡ over the folder that now contains the file and then press the left button.

◆ The contents of the folder appear, displaying the file you moved.

You can delete a file in Windows Explorer that you no longer need.

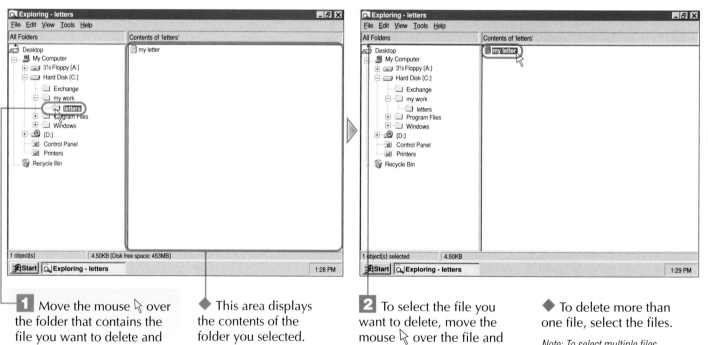

1 Move the mouse ⟍ over the folder that contains the file you want to delete and then press the left button.

◆ This area displays the contents of the folder you selected.

2 To select the file you want to delete, move the mouse ⟍ over the file and then press the left button.

◆ To delete more than one file, select the files.

Note: To select multiple files, refer to page 85.

- Start Windows Explorer
- Display or Hide Folders
- Create a New Folder
- Move a File to Another Folder
- Delete a File

IMPORTANT!

You can also open, preview, print and rename files in Windows Explorer.

Note: For information on performing these tasks, refer to the Work With Files and Folders chapter, starting on page 84.

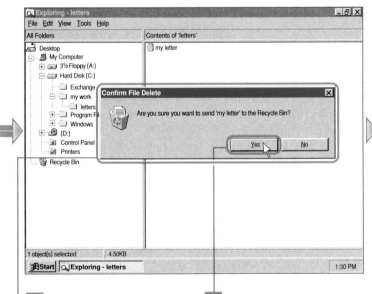

3 Press Delete on your keyboard and the **Confirm File Delete** dialog box appears.

4 To delete the file, move the mouse ⌀ over **Yes** and then press the left button.

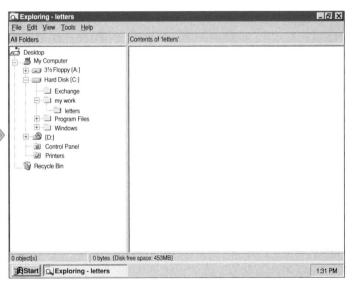

◆ The file disappears.

Note: You can restore a file you have deleted. For more information, refer to page 104.

DELETE A FOLDER

To select the folder you want to delete, move the mouse ⌀ over the folder and then press the left button. Then perform steps **3** and **4**.

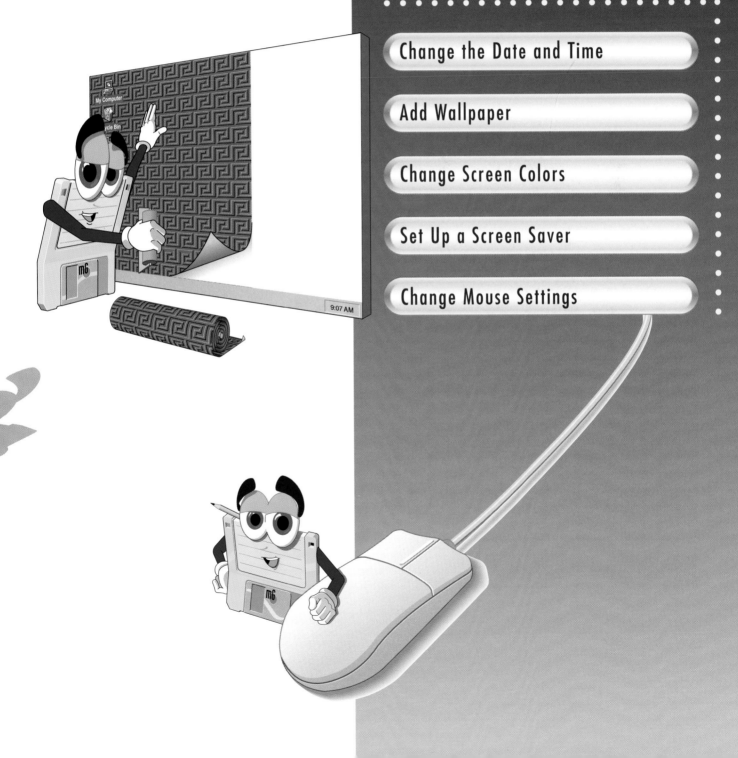

CHANGE WINDOWS SETTINGS

- Change the Date and Time
- Add Wallpaper
- Change Screen Colors
- Set Up a Screen Saver
- Change Mouse Settings

It is important to have the correct date and time set in your computer. Windows uses this information to identify each document you create or update.

CHANGE THE DATE AND TIME

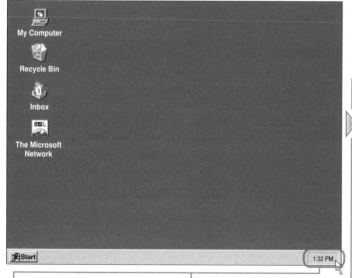

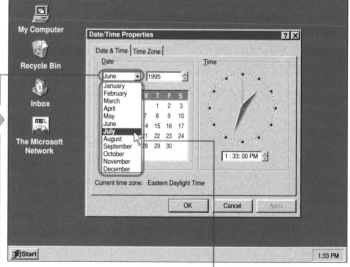

◆ This area displays the time set in your computer.

1 To change the date or time set in your computer, move the mouse ▷ over this area and then quickly press the left button twice.

◆ The **Date/Time Properties** dialog box appears.

◆ This area displays the month set in your computer.

2 To change the month, move the mouse ▷ over this area and then press the left button.

3 Move the mouse ▷ over the correct month (example: **July**) and then press the left button.

- **Change the Date and Time**
- Add Wallpaper
- Change Screen Colors
- Set Up a Screen Saver
- Change Mouse Settings

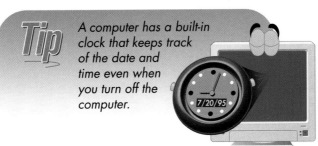

A computer has a built-in clock that keeps track of the date and time even when you turn off the computer.

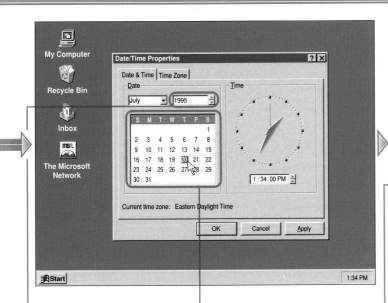

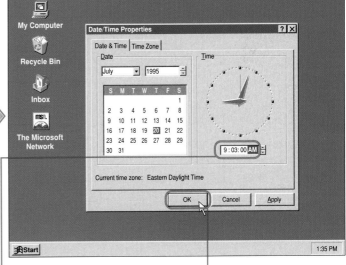

◆ This area displays the year set in your computer.

4 To change the year, move the mouse ⬏ over ▲ or ▼ and then press the left button until the correct year appears (example: **1995**).

◆ This area displays the days in the month. The current day is highlighted.

5 To change the day, move the mouse ⬏ over the correct day (example: **20**) and then press the left button.

◆ This area displays the time set in your computer.

6 To change the time, move the mouse I over the part of the time you want to change and then quickly press the left button twice. Then type the correct information.

7 To apply the date and time changes you made, move the mouse ⬏ over **OK** and then press the left button.

127

ADD WALLPAPER

You can decorate your screen by adding wallpaper.

9:07 AM

ADD WALLPAPER

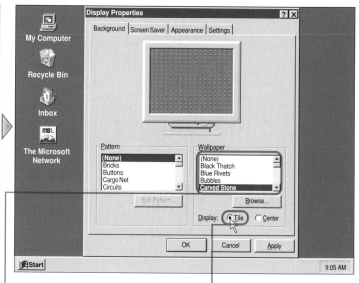

1 Move the mouse ⟍ over a blank area on your screen and then press the **right** button. A menu appears.

2 Move the mouse ⟍ over **Properties** and then press the left button.

◆ The **Display Properties** dialog box appears.

3 Move the mouse ⟍ over the wallpaper you want to display (example: **Carved Stone**) and then press the left button.

Note: To view all the available wallpapers, use the scroll bar. For more information, refer to page 32.

4 To cover your entire screen with the wallpaper you selected, move the mouse ⟍ over **Tile** and then press the left button (○ changes to ⊙).

*Note: To place a small wallpaper image in the middle of your screen, select the **Center** option.*

- Change the Date and Time
- **Add Wallpaper**
- Change Screen Colors
- Set Up a Screen Saver
- Change Mouse Settings

These are a few of the available wallpapers.

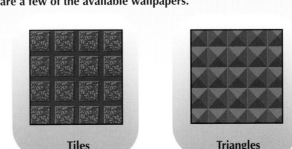

Straw Mat   Tiles   Triangles

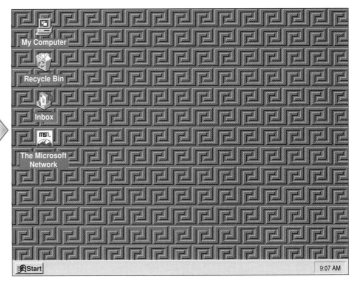

◆ This area displays how the wallpaper you selected will look on your screen.

5 To display the wallpaper on your screen, move the mouse over **OK** and then press the left button.

◆ Your screen displays the wallpaper you selected.

Note: To remove wallpaper from your screen, perform steps **1** *to* **3**, *selecting **(None)** in step* **3**. *Then perform step* **5**.

You can change the colors displayed on your screen to suit your preferences.

CHANGE SCREEN COLORS

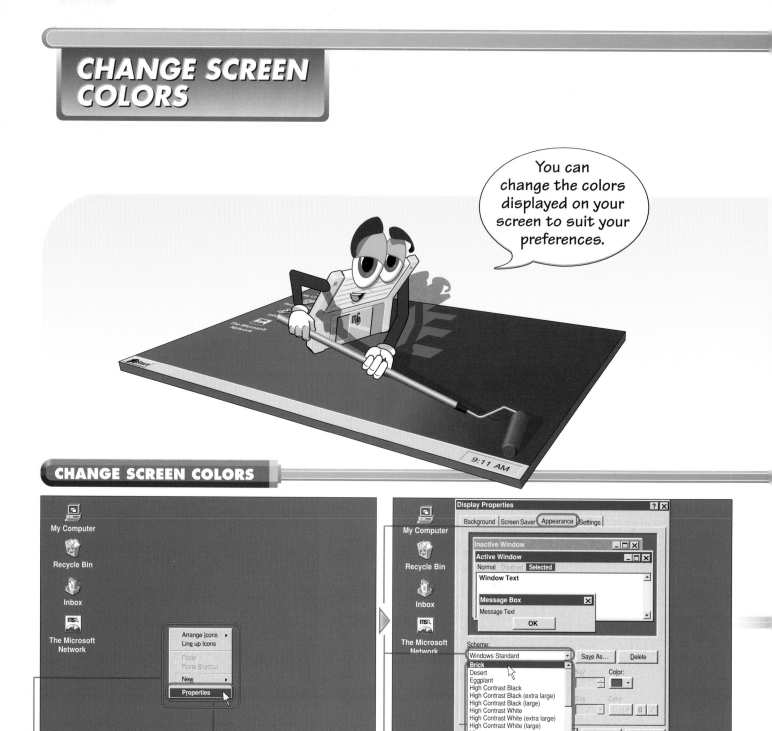

1 Move the mouse ℝ over a blank area on your screen and then press the **right** button. A menu appears.

2 Move the mouse ℝ over **Properties** and then press the left button.

◆ The **Display Properties** dialog box appears.

3 Move the mouse ℝ over the **Appearance** tab and then press the left button.

4 To display a list of the available color schemes, move the mouse ℝ over this area and then press the left button.

5 Move the mouse ℝ over the color scheme you want to use (example: **Brick**) and then press the left button.

Note: To view all the available color schemes, use the scroll bar. For more information, refer to page 32.

- Change the Date and Time
- Add Wallpaper
- **Change Screen Colors**
- Set Up a Screen Saver
- Change Mouse Settings

Message Box
Message Text
OK

Wheat

These are a few
of the available
color schemes.

Message Box
Message Text
OK

Rose

Message Box
Message Text
OK

Teal (VGA)

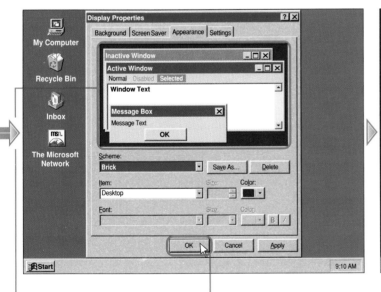

◆ This area displays how your screen will look with the color scheme you selected.

6 To apply the color scheme, move the mouse over **OK** and then press the left button.

◆ Your screen displays the color scheme you selected.

Note: To return to the original color scheme, repeat steps **1** *to* **6**, *selecting **Windows Standard** in step* **5**.

A screen saver is a moving picture or pattern that appears on the screen when you do not use your computer for a period of time.

SET UP A SCREEN SAVER

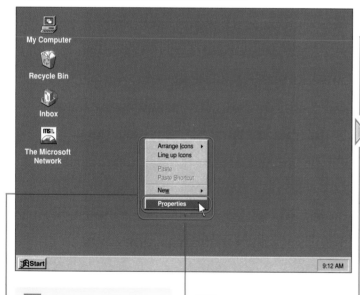

1 Move the mouse ⌖ over a blank area on your screen and then press the **right** button. A menu appears.

2 Move the mouse ⌖ over **Properties** and then press the left button.

◆ The **Display Properties** dialog box appears.

3 Move the mouse ⌖ over the **Screen Saver** tab and then press the left button.

4 Move the mouse ⌖ over this area and then press the left button.

5 Move the mouse ⌖ over **Flying Windows** and then press the left button.

Note: Windows provides screen savers that are not part of the basic installation. You can add these screen savers at any time.

- Change the Date and Time
- Add Wallpaper
- Change Screen Colors
- **Set Up a Screen Saver**
- Change Mouse Settings

Screen savers were originally designed to prevent screen burn, which occurs when an image appears in a fixed position for a period of time.

Today's monitors are better designed to prevent screen burn, but people still use screen savers for entertainment.

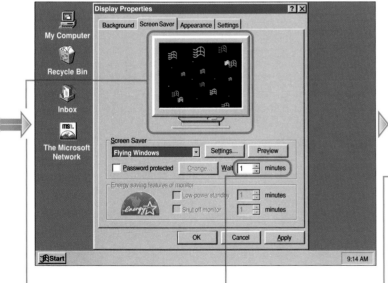

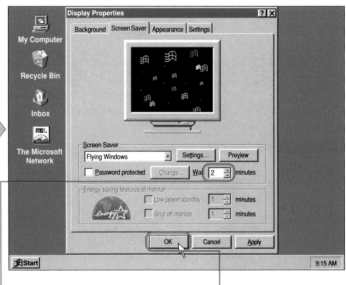

◆ This area displays how the screen saver will look on your screen.

◆ The screen saver will appear when you do not use your computer for the amount of time displayed in this area.

6 To change the amount of time, move the mouse I over this area and then press the left button.

7 Press **←Backspace** or **Delete** to remove the existing number. Then type a new number.

8 Move the mouse ⌖ over **OK** and then press the left button.

CHANGE MOUSE SETTINGS

You can change the way your mouse works to suit your needs.

CHANGE MOUSE SETTINGS

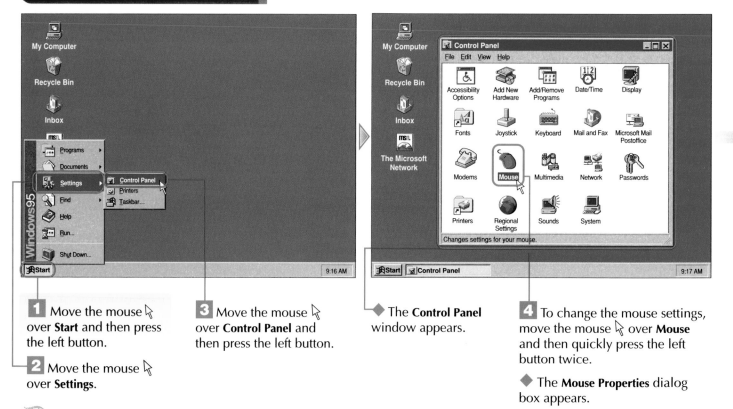

1 Move the mouse over **Start** and then press the left button.

2 Move the mouse over **Settings**.

3 Move the mouse over **Control Panel** and then press the left button.

◆ The **Control Panel** window appears.

4 To change the mouse settings, move the mouse over **Mouse** and then quickly press the left button twice.

◆ The **Mouse Properties** dialog box appears.

- Change the Date and Time
- Add Wallpaper
- Change Screen Colors
- Set Up a Screen Saver
- **Change Mouse Settings**

A mouse pad provides a smooth surface for moving a mouse on your desk. You can buy mouse pads displaying interesting designs or pictures at most computer stores.

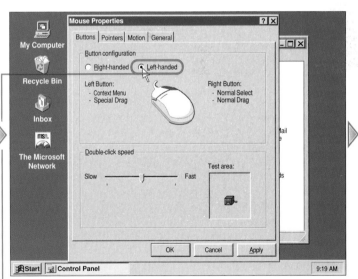

SWITCH BUTTONS

If you are left-handed, you can switch the functions of the left and right mouse buttons to make the mouse easier to use.

◆ This area describes the current functions of the left and right mouse buttons.

1 To switch the functions of the buttons, move the mouse � over this option and then press the left button (O changes to ◉).

Note: This change will not take effect until you confirm the changes. To do so, refer to page 137.

135

CHANGE MOUSE SETTINGS

You can personalize your mouse by changing the double-click speed and the way the mouse pointer moves on your screen.

CHANGE MOUSE SETTINGS (CONTINUED)

DOUBLE-CLICK SPEED

You can change the amount of time that can pass between two clicks of the mouse button for Windows to recognize a double-click.

1 To change the double-click speed, move the mouse ⬚ over ⬚.

2 Press and hold down the left button as you drag ⬚ to increase or decrease the double-click speed. Then release the button.

3 To test the double-click speed, move the mouse ⬚ over this area and then quickly press the left button twice.

◆ The jack-in-the-box appears if you clicked at the correct speed.

Note: If you are an inexperienced mouse user, you may find a slower speed easier to use.

- Change the Date and Time
- Add Wallpaper
- Change Screen Colors
- Set Up a Screen Saver
- **Change Mouse Settings**

Tip

Displaying mouse trails can help you follow the movement of the mouse on your screen. This is especially useful on portable computer screens, where the mouse can be difficult to follow.

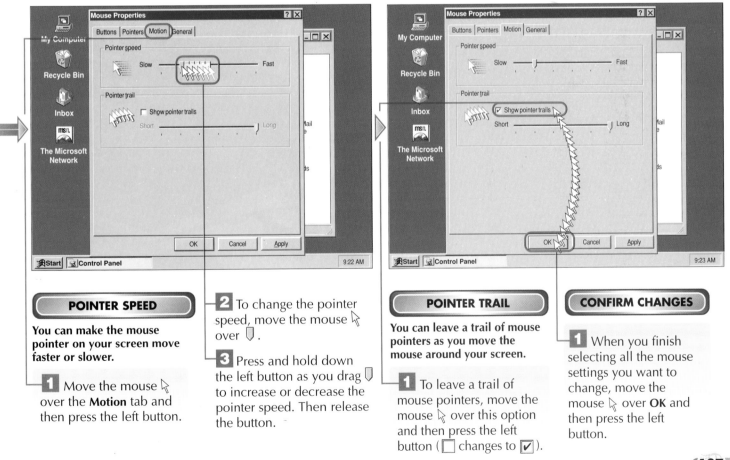

POINTER SPEED

You can make the mouse pointer on your screen move faster or slower.

1 Move the mouse ⌖ over the **Motion** tab and then press the left button.

2 To change the pointer speed, move the mouse ⌖ over ⬇.

3 Press and hold down the left button as you drag ⬇ to increase or decrease the pointer speed. Then release the button.

POINTER TRAIL

You can leave a trail of mouse pointers as you move the mouse around your screen.

1 To leave a trail of mouse pointers, move the mouse ⌖ over this option and then press the left button (☐ changes to ☑).

CONFIRM CHANGES

1 When you finish selecting all the mouse settings you want to change, move the mouse ⌖ over **OK** and then press the left button.

137

START MICROSOFT EXCHANGE

Microsoft Exchange lets you send and receive faxes and electronic mail (e-mail).

START MICROSOFT EXCHANGE

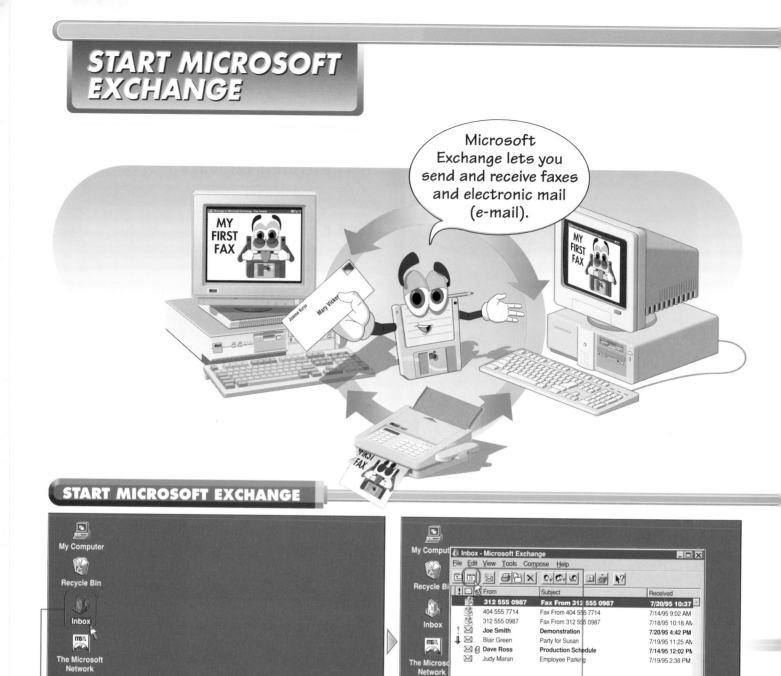

1 Move the mouse ⟋ over **Inbox** and then quickly press the left button twice.

*Note: If the **Inbox** is not displayed on your screen, you must install the Microsoft Exchange and Microsoft Fax programs to continue.*

◆ The **Microsoft Exchange** window appears.

2 To display the folders that store your messages, move the mouse ⟋ over ▣ and then press the left button.

- **Start Microsoft Exchange**
- Send a Fax
- Change How Modem Answers Faxes
- View a Fax
- Print a Fax

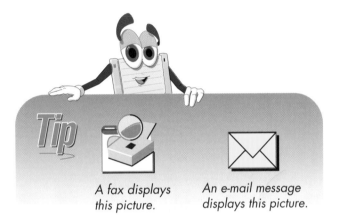

A fax displays
this picture.

An e-mail message
displays this picture.

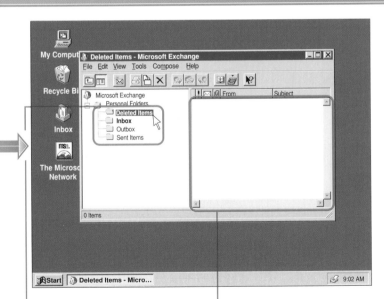

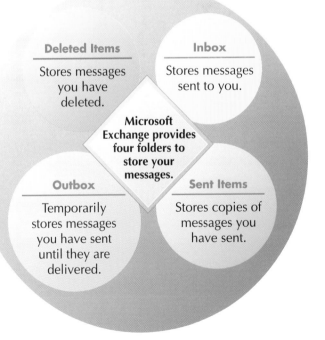

Deleted Items

Stores messages
you have
deleted.

Inbox

Stores messages
sent to you.

Microsoft
Exchange provides
four folders to
store your
messages.

Outbox

Temporarily
stores messages
you have sent
until they are
delivered.

Sent Items

Stores copies of
messages you
have sent.

◆ The folders appear.

3 To display the contents of a folder, move the mouse over the folder and then press the left button.

◆ This area displays the contents of the folder you selected. You can only display the contents of one folder at a time.

Note: In this example, there are no messages in the Deleted Items folder.

You can easily send a fax to a colleague across the city or around the world.

◆ To start **Microsoft Exchange**, refer to page 140.

1 Move the mouse ▷ over **Compose** and then press the left button.

2 Move the mouse ▷ over **New Fax** and then press the left button.

◆ The **Compose New Fax** dialog box appears.

3 Move the mouse ▷ over **Next** and then press the left button.

- Start Microsoft Exchange
- **Send a Fax**
- Change How Modem Answers Faxes
- View a Fax
- Print a Fax

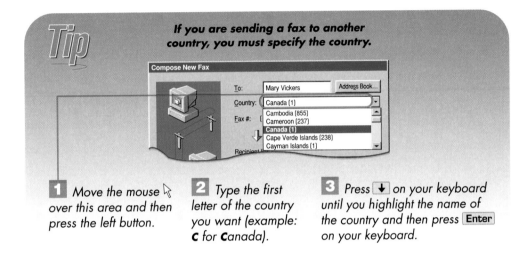

If you are sending a fax to another country, you must specify the country.

1 Move the mouse ᐟ over this area and then press the left button.

2 Type the first letter of the country you want (example: **C** for **C**anada).

3 Press ⬇ on your keyboard until you highlight the name of the country and then press **Enter** on your keyboard.

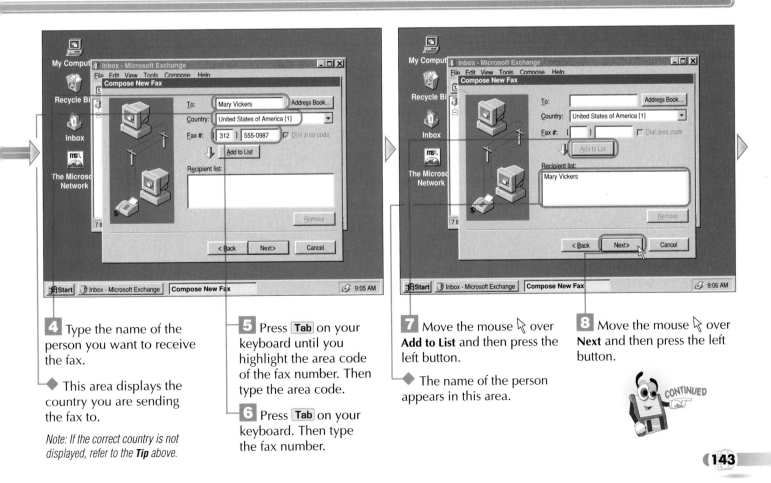

4 Type the name of the person you want to receive the fax.

◆ This area displays the country you are sending the fax to.

Note: If the correct country is not displayed, refer to the **Tip** above.

5 Press **Tab** on your keyboard until you highlight the area code of the fax number. Then type the area code.

6 Press **Tab** on your keyboard. Then type the fax number.

7 Move the mouse ᐟ over **Add to List** and then press the left button.

◆ The name of the person appears in this area.

8 Move the mouse ᐟ over **Next** and then press the left button.

CONTINUED

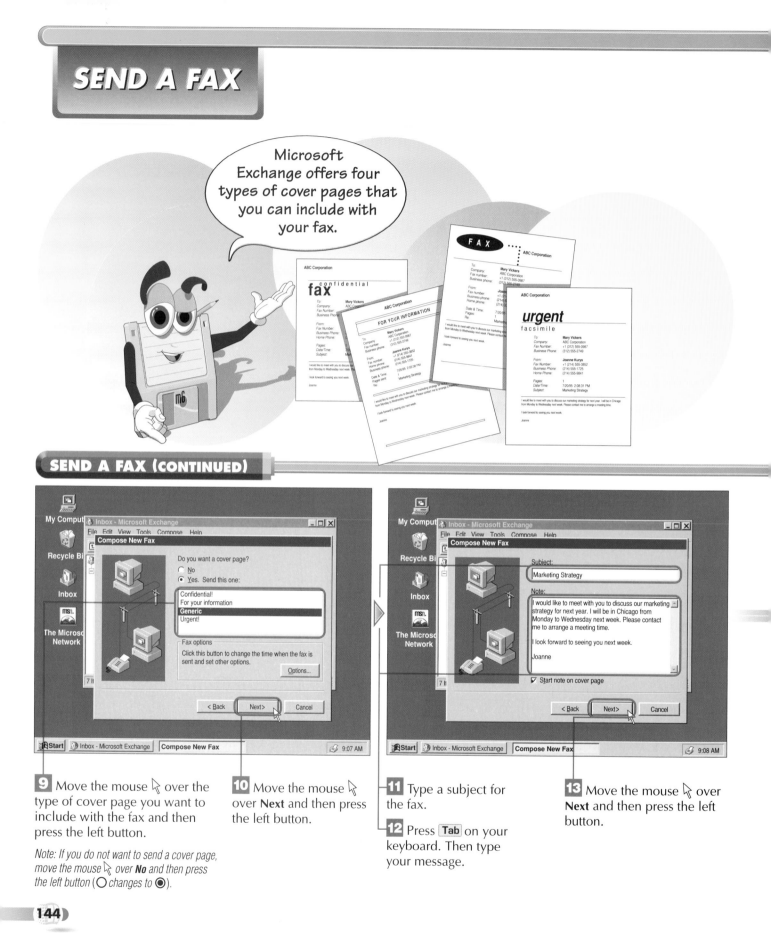

Microsoft Exchange offers four types of cover pages that you can include with your fax.

SEND A FAX (CONTINUED)

9 Move the mouse ⌖ over the type of cover page you want to include with the fax and then press the left button.

*Note: If you do not want to send a cover page, move the mouse ⌖ over **No** and then press the left button (○ changes to ◉).*

10 Move the mouse ⌖ over **Next** and then press the left button.

11 Type a subject for the fax.

12 Press **Tab** on your keyboard. Then type your message.

13 Move the mouse ⌖ over **Next** and then press the left button.

- Start Microsoft Exchange
- **Send a Fax**
- Change How Modem Answers Faxes
- View a Fax
- Print a Fax

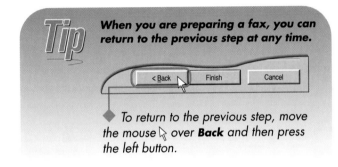

When you are preparing a fax, you can return to the previous step at any time.

◆ To return to the previous step, move the mouse ▷ over **Back** and then press the left button.

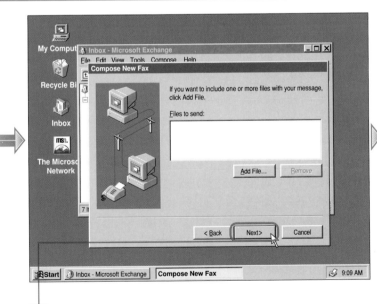

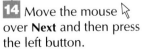

14 Move the mouse ▷ over **Next** and then press the left button.

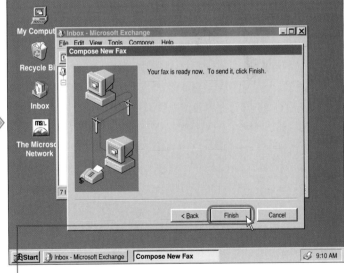

15 To send the fax, move the mouse ▷ over **Finish** and then press the left button.

CHANGE HOW MODEM ANSWERS FAXES

You can instruct your modem to answer incoming faxes in the way that is most convenient for you.

CHANGE HOW MODEM ANSWERS FAXES

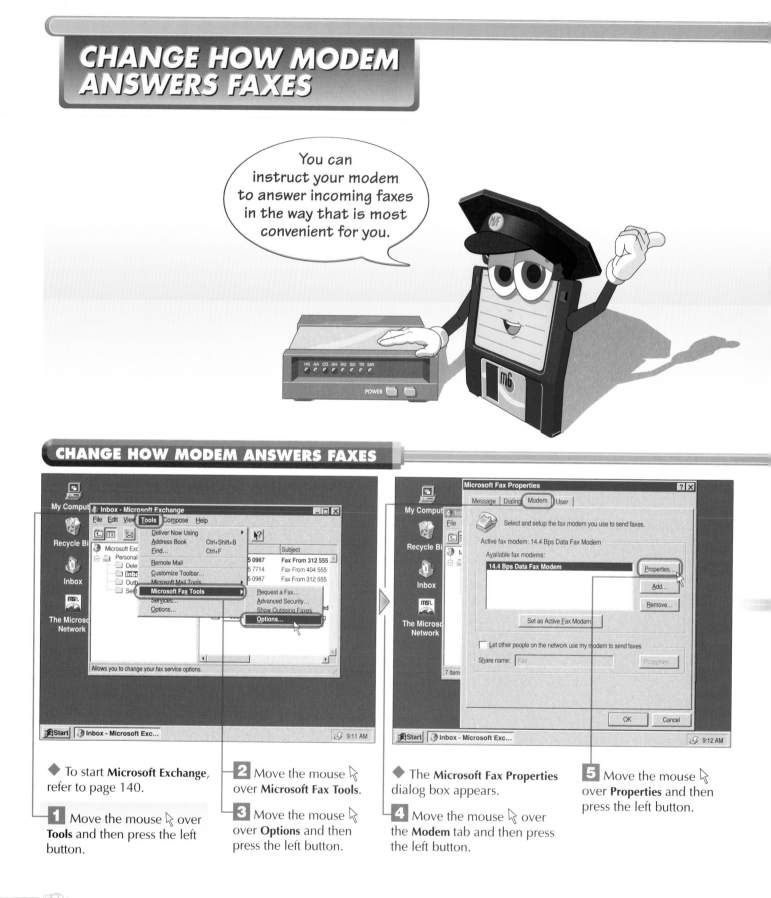

◆ To start **Microsoft Exchange**, refer to page 140.

1 Move the mouse ⌖ over **Tools** and then press the left button.

2 Move the mouse ⌖ over **Microsoft Fax Tools**.

3 Move the mouse ⌖ over **Options** and then press the left button.

◆ The **Microsoft Fax Properties** dialog box appears.

4 Move the mouse ⌖ over the **Modem** tab and then press the left button.

5 Move the mouse ⌖ over **Properties** and then press the left button.

146

- Start Microsoft Exchange
- Send a Fax
- **Change How Modem Answers Faxes**
- View a Fax
- Print a Fax

Answer after

The modem will answer all incoming faxes after the number of rings you specify. Select this option if you use the telephone line primarily for faxing.

Manual

The modem will only answer incoming faxes when you instruct it to. Select this option if you use the telephone line primarily for voice calls.

Note: A dialog box appears when someone is sending you a fax.
*To answer the fax, move the mouse over **Yes** and then press the left button.*

Don't answer

The modem will not answer incoming faxes.

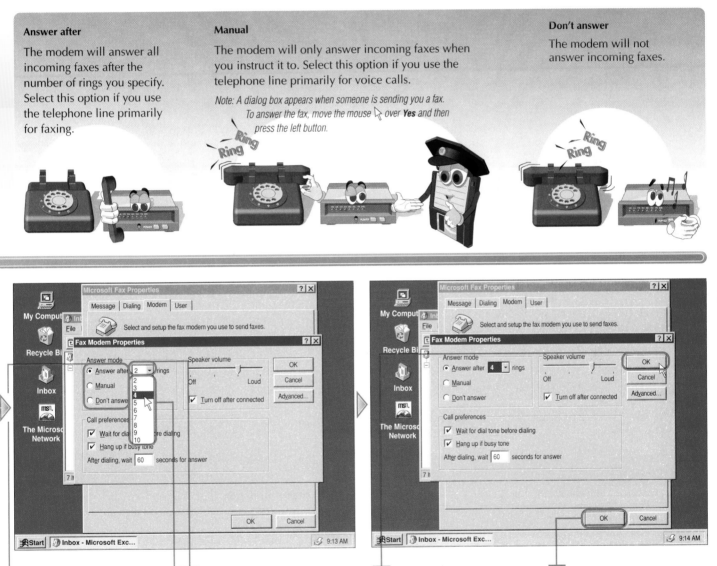

◆ The **Fax Modem Properties** dialog box appears.

6 Move the mouse over the answering option you want and then press the left button (○ changes to ●).

7 If you selected **Answer after** in step **6**, move the mouse over this area and then press the left button.

8 Move the mouse over the number of times you want the telephone line to ring before the modem answers and then press the left button.

9 To close the **Fax Modem Properties** dialog box, move the mouse over **OK** and then press the left button.

10 To close the **Microsoft Fax Properties** dialog box, move the mouse over **OK** and then press the left button.

> You can display a fax on your screen so you can read the message.

To receive a fax, you must have Microsoft Exchange running. To start Microsoft Exchange, refer to page 140.

VIEW A FAX

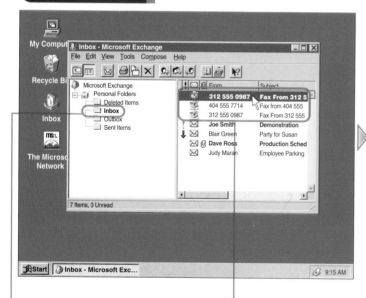

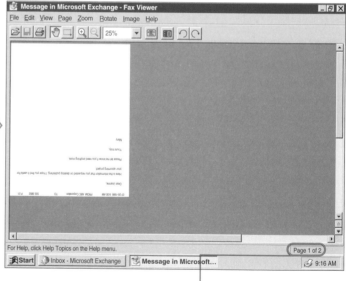

◆ To start **Microsoft Exchange**, refer to page 140.

1 To display the faxes sent to you, move the mouse ⟍ over the **Inbox** folder and then press the left button.

2 Move the mouse ⟍ over the fax you want to view and then quickly press the left button twice.

Note: A fax displays the 📧 *picture.*

◆ The **Fax Viewer** window appears, displaying the first page of the fax.

Note: To enlarge the window to fill your screen, refer to page 16.

◆ This area indicates which page is displayed and the total number of pages in the fax.

- Start Microsoft Exchange
- Send a Fax
- Change How Modem Answers Faxes
- View a Fax
- Print a Fax

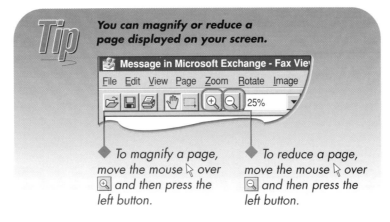

Tip

You can magnify or reduce a page displayed on your screen.

◆ To magnify a page, move the mouse ⏥ over 🔍 and then press the left button.

◆ To reduce a page, move the mouse ⏥ over 🔍 and then press the left button.

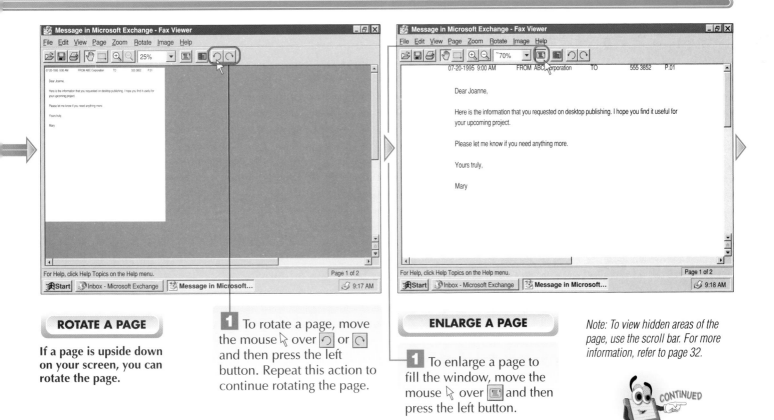

ROTATE A PAGE

If a page is upside down on your screen, you can rotate the page.

1 To rotate a page, move the mouse ⏥ over 🔄 or 🔄 and then press the left button. Repeat this action to continue rotating the page.

ENLARGE A PAGE

1 To enlarge a page to fill the window, move the mouse ⏥ over 🖼 and then press the left button.

Note: To view hidden areas of the page, use the scroll bar. For more information, refer to page 32.

CONTINUED

The Fax Viewer window lets you display a small version of each page in a fax.

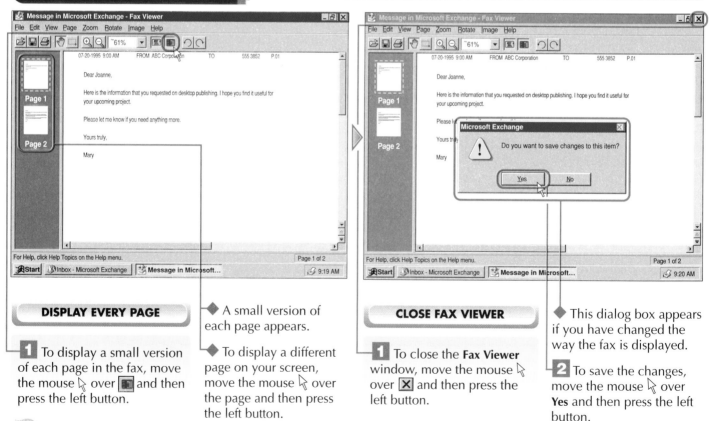

DISPLAY EVERY PAGE

1 To display a small version of each page in the fax, move the mouse ⬉ over 🔲 and then press the left button.

◆ A small version of each page appears.

◆ To display a different page on your screen, move the mouse ⬉ over the page and then press the left button.

CLOSE FAX VIEWER

1 To close the **Fax Viewer** window, move the mouse ⬉ over ⊠ and then press the left button.

◆ This dialog box appears if you have changed the way the fax is displayed.

2 To save the changes, move the mouse ⬉ over **Yes** and then press the left button.

- Start Microsoft Exchange
- Send a Fax
- Change How Modem Answers Faxes
- **View a Fax**
- **Print a Fax**

You can easily produce a paper copy of a fax you received.

PRINT A FAX

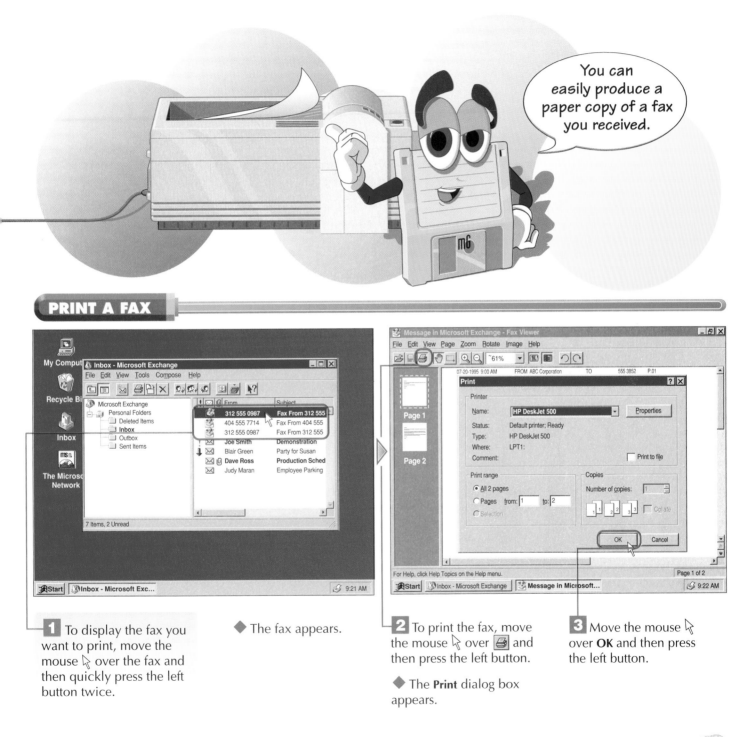

1 To display the fax you want to print, move the mouse ⌖ over the fax and then quickly press the left button twice.

◆ The fax appears.

2 To print the fax, move the mouse ⌖ over 🖨 and then press the left button.

◆ The **Print** dialog box appears.

3 Move the mouse ⌖ over **OK** and then press the left button.

THE MICROSOFT NETWORK

Introduction

Connect to The Microsoft Network

Select a Topic Area

Exit The Microsoft Network

MSN TODAY

E - MAIL

FAVORITE PLACES

MEMBER ASSISTANCE

CATEGORIES

INTRODUCTION

The Microsoft Network (MSN) provides a vast amount of information and allows you to communicate with people around the world.

CHAT WITH OTHER MEMBERS

The Microsoft Network lets you have conversations with other members. You can observe ongoing conversations or make comments and ask questions that other members will see immediately.

EXCHANGE ELECTRONIC MAIL

You can exchange private messages with millions of people around the world. This includes MSN members, members of other online services and anyone using the Internet.

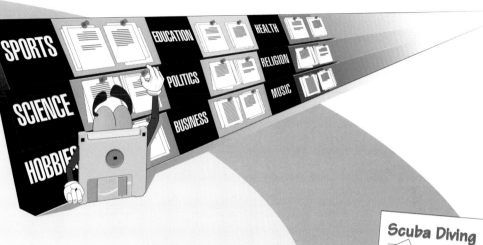

BULLETIN BOARD SERVICES (BBS)

You can read and post (send) messages on public bulletin boards. A bulletin board is an area where you can communicate with other MSN members with similar interests. Bulletin board topics include sports, education, science, business, entertainment, hobbies and much more.

TRANSFER FILES

MSN provides thousands of useful files, such as documents, pictures and programs, that you can copy (download) to your computer.

Note: There may be a fee for copying some files.

INTERNET

You can exchange electronic messages with anyone connected to the Internet. You can also access thousands of newsgroups. Each newsgroup discusses a specific topic and allows people with common interests to communicate with each other. Windsurfing, politics, anthropology, religion, the environment, education and health are just a few of the newsgroup topics available.

Note: Newsgroups are similar to MSN bulletin boards, except they are available to everyone connected to the Internet.

CONNECT TO THE MICROSOFT NETWORK

msn
You must connect to The Microsoft Network to use the services it provides.

CONNECT TO THE MICROSOFT NETWORK

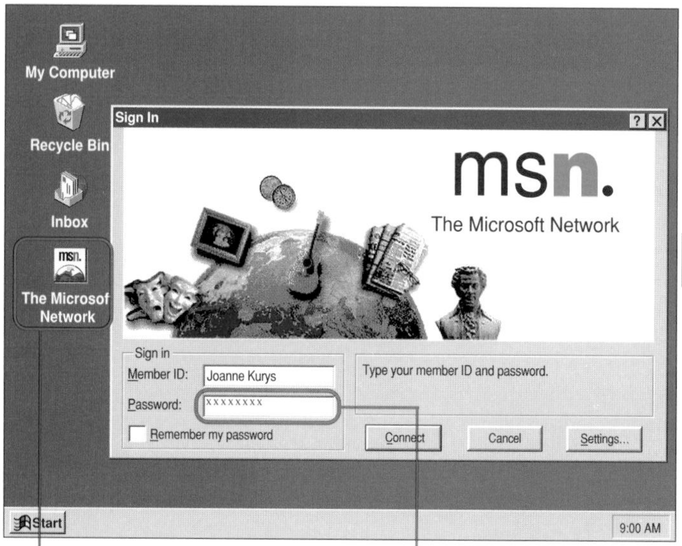
My Computer
Recycle Bin
Inbox
The Microsoft Network
Sign In
msn.
The Microsoft Network
Sign in
Member ID: Joanne Kurys
Password: xxxxxxxx
Remember my password
Type your member ID and password.
Connect
Cancel
Settings...
Start
9:00 AM

MSN Today
File Help
MSN TODAY
CALENDAR OF EVENTS
GO TO...
msn.
MSN TODAY
Russell Siegelman chat
Join the GM of Microsoft Online Services at 4:00 PM (PDT), Thursday, June 22, in the Special Events folder, Babbage Auditorium. Click his picture to go there now.
Interactive Media Conference
Find out how to be a part of the Microsoft Interactive Media Conference taking place July 18-20. Click the graphic to find out more.
UN 50th Anniversary Forum
United Nations
Celebrate the 50th Anniversary of the formation of the United Nations. Click the icon at left to discover more.
Hey, there's more! See the Calendar of Events for a list of the many other events happening today and everyday on MSN.
Start
The Microsoft Network
MSN Today

1 Move the mouse ↖ over this icon and then quickly press the left button twice.

◆ The **Sign In** dialog box appears.

2 Type your password and then press **Enter** on your keyboard.

Note: A symbol (x) appears for each character you type.

◆ The **MSN Today** window appears, displaying upcoming events on The Microsoft Network.

3 To close the window, move the mouse ↖ over ☒ and then press the left button.

This dialog box appears if you are not connected to The Microsoft Network.

To connect to The Microsoft Network, follow the instructions in the dialog box.

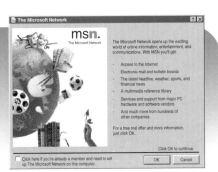

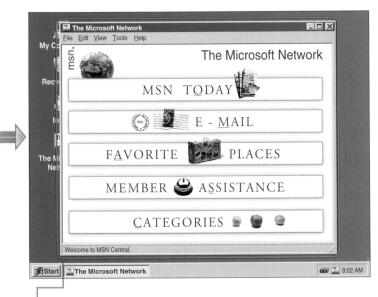

◆ The Microsoft Network main window appears, displaying the five main topic areas available on the network.

Note: To select a topic area, refer to the next page.

There are five main topic areas on The Microsoft Network.

MSN TODAY	Provides new information about The Microsoft Network.
E-MAIL	Lets you send and receive electronic mail.
FAVORITE PLACES	Lets you quickly access the services on The Microsoft Network that you use most often.
MEMBER ASSISTANCE	Provides help to members of The Microsoft Network.
CATEGORIES	Lets you browse through the information on The Microsoft Network.

You can select a topic area on The Microsoft Network to view the information it provides.

SELECT A TOPIC AREA

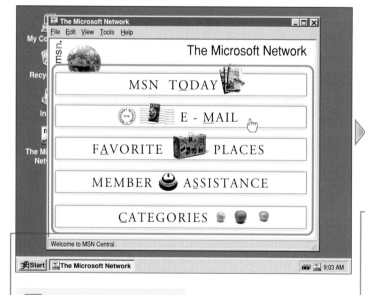

1 To select a topic area, move the mouse 🖑 over the area (example: **E-MAIL**) and then press the left button.

◆ A window appears, displaying information for the topic area you selected.

Note: To close a window, move the mouse ▷ over ✖ and then press the left button.

You can disconnect from The Microsoft Network when you no longer want to use the information and services it provides.

EXIT THE MICROSOFT NETWORK

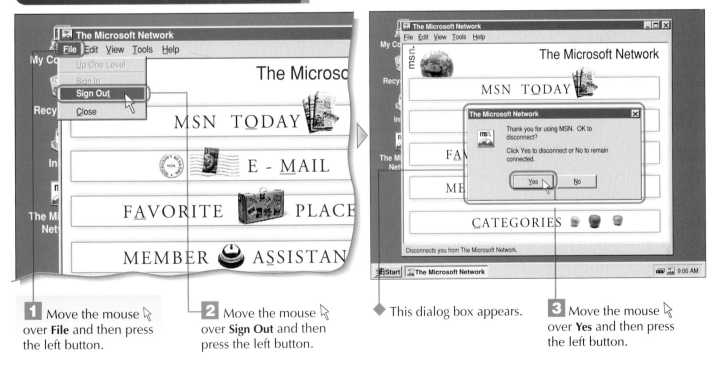

1 Move the mouse ⌖ over **File** and then press the left button.

2 Move the mouse ⌖ over **Sign Out** and then press the left button.

◆ This dialog box appears.

3 Move the mouse ⌖ over **Yes** and then press the left button.

ELECTRONIC MAIL

- Add Name to Address Book
- Send a Message
- Insert a File in a Message
- Delete a Message
- Read a Message
- Reply to a Message
- Forward a Message

Message

ADD NAME TO ADDRESS BOOK

Microsoft Exchange provides a personal address book where you can store the names and addresses of people you frequently send messages to.

ADD NAME TO ADDRESS BOOK

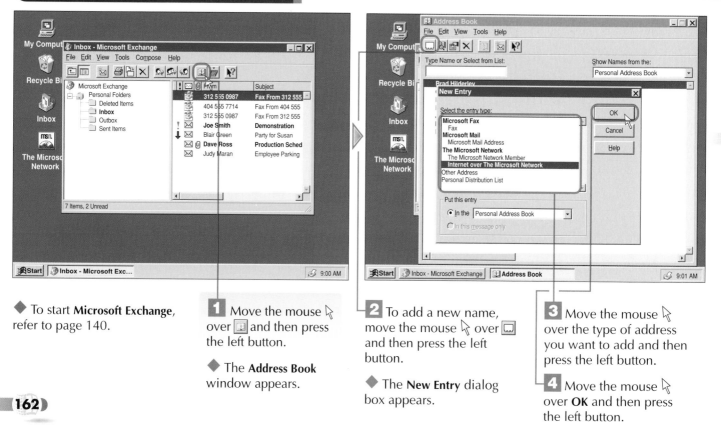

◆ To start **Microsoft Exchange**, refer to page 140.

1 Move the mouse ⌖ over 🔲 and then press the left button.

◆ The **Address Book** window appears.

2 To add a new name, move the mouse ⌖ over 🔲 and then press the left button.

◆ The **New Entry** dialog box appears.

3 Move the mouse ⌖ over the type of address you want to add and then press the left button.

4 Move the mouse ⌖ over **OK** and then press the left button.

162

- • **Add Name to Address Book**
- • Send a Message
- • Insert a File in a Message
- • Delete a Message
- • Read a Message
- • Reply to a Message
- • Forward a Message

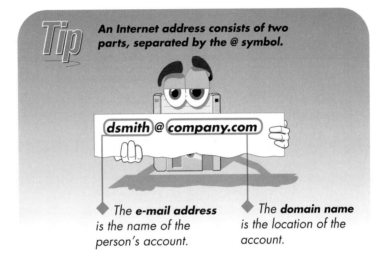

An Internet address consists of two parts, separated by the @ symbol.

dsmith @ company.com

◆ The **e-mail address** is the name of the person's account.

◆ The **domain name** is the location of the account.

5 Type the information that corresponds to the first box and then press **Tab** on your keyboard.

Note: The appearance of this dialog box varies, depending on the type of address you selected in step **3**.

6 Repeat step **5** until you have entered all the information.

7 Move the mouse over **OK** and then press the left button.

8 To close the **Address Book** window, move the mouse over ✖ and then press the left button.

You can send a message to another person to exchange ideas or request information.

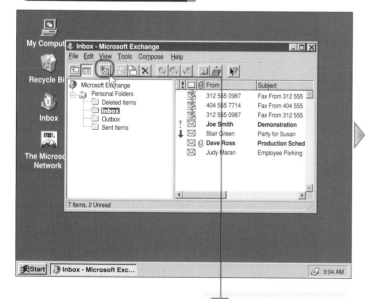

◆ To start **Microsoft Exchange**, refer to page 140.

1 Move the mouse over 🖂 and then press the left button.

◆ The **New Message** window appears.

2 To send the message to a person listed in an address book, move the mouse over **To** and then press the left button.

*Note: You can also type the e-mail address of the person you want to receive the message in the **To** box (example: **dsmith@company.com**). This lets you skip steps **2** to **7**.*

◆ The **Address Book** dialog box appears.

- Add Name to Address Book
- **Send a Message**
- Insert a File in a Message
- Delete a Message
- Read a Message
- Reply to a Message
- Forward a Message

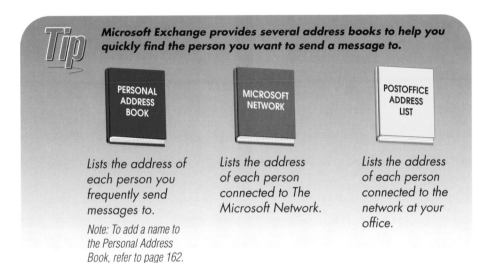

Microsoft Exchange provides several address books to help you quickly find the person you want to send a message to.

PERSONAL ADDRESS BOOK — Lists the address of each person you frequently send messages to.

Note: To add a name to the Personal Address Book, refer to page 162.

MICROSOFT NETWORK — Lists the address of each person connected to The Microsoft Network.

POSTOFFICE ADDRESS LIST — Lists the address of each person connected to the network at your office.

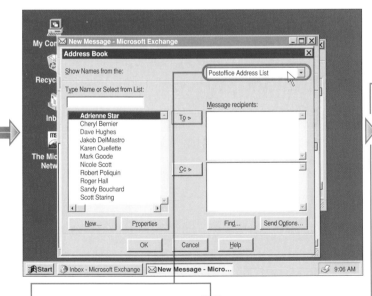

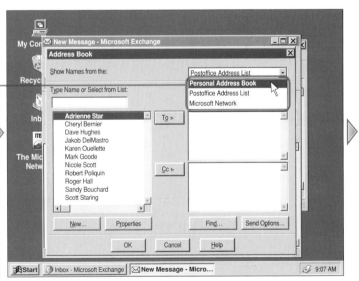

◆ This area displays the name of the address book currently displayed.

Note: For information on address books, refer to the **Tip** above.

3 To display the names from a different address book, move the mouse over this area and then press the left button.

4 Move the mouse over the name of the address book you want to display and then press the left button.

CONTINUED

When sending a message, you should enter a subject that will help the reader quickly identify the contents of your message.

Subject: Financial Statement

SEND A MESSAGE (CONTINUED)

5 Move the mouse ⊳ over the name of the person you want to receive the message and then press the left button.

6 Move the mouse ⊳ over **To** and then press the left button.

◆ This area displays the name of the person you selected.

*Note: To send the message to more than one person, repeat steps **5** and **6** for each person.*

7 Move the mouse ⊳ over **OK** and then press the left button.

- Add Name to Address Book
- **Send a Message**
- Insert a File in a Message
- Delete a Message

- Read a Message
- Reply to a Message
- Forward a Message

Tip

You can use Microsoft Exchange to send messages to co-workers, other members of The Microsoft Network, members of other online services and anyone using the Internet.

8 To enter a subject for the message, move the mouse I over the area beside **Subject:** and then press the left button. Then type the subject of the message.

9 To enter the message, move the mouse I over this area and then press the left button. Then type the message.

10 To indicate the importance of the message, move the mouse over one of the following options and then press the left button.

High priority

Low priority

11 To send the message, move the mouse over and then press the left button.

Note: If you are sending the message over The Microsoft Network, you must connect to the network. To do so, refer to page 156.

INSERT A FILE IN A MESSAGE

You can insert a file in a message. This is useful when you want to include additional information.

INSERT A FILE IN A MESSAGE

1 To create a message, perform steps **1** to **10** starting on page 164.

2 Move the mouse I over the area where you want to place the file and then press the left button.

3 Move the mouse over [U] and then press the left button.

- Add Name to Address Book
- Send a Message
- Insert a File in a Message
- Delete a Message

- Read a Message
- Reply to a Message
- Forward a Message

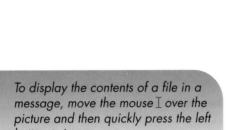

Tip

To display the contents of a file in a message, move the mouse I over the picture and then quickly press the left button twice.

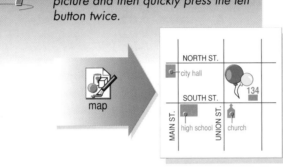

◆ The **Insert File** dialog box appears.

4 Move the mouse ↖ over the file you want to include with the message and then press the left button.

5 Move the mouse ↖ over **OK** and then press the left button.

◆ The name of the file and a small picture appear in the message.

6 To send the message, move the mouse ↖ over ✉ and then press the left button.

Note: If you are sending the message over The Microsoft Network, you must connect to the network. To do so, refer to page 156.

You can delete messages you no longer need.

DELETE A MESSAGE

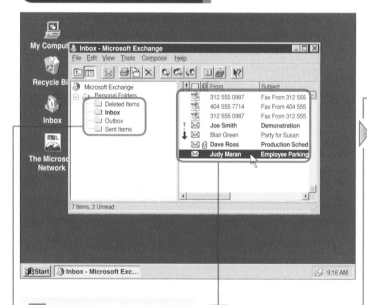

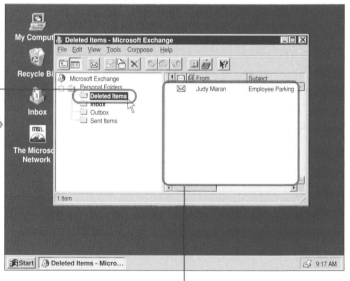

1 Move the mouse ⌖ over the folder that contains the message you want to delete (example: **Inbox**) and then press the left button.

2 Move the mouse ⌖ over the message and then press the left button.

3 Press Delete on your keyboard and Microsoft Exchange places the message in the **Deleted Items** folder.

4 To view the messages you have deleted, move the mouse ⌖ over the **Deleted Items** folder and then press the left button.

◆ This area displays the messages you have deleted.

*Note: Deleting a message from the **Deleted Items** folder will permanently remove the message from your computer.*

- Add Name to Address Book
- Send a Message
- Insert a File in a Message
- Delete a Message

- Read a Message
- Reply to a Message
- Forward a Message

You can easily display a message sent to you. Each message displays a symbol to provide additional information.

! ✉ High Priority Message

✉ Normal Priority Message

↓ ✉ Low Priority Message

✉ 🗐 Message with an attached file

🖹 Faxed Message

READ A MESSAGE

1 Move the mouse ⇖ over the **Inbox** folder and then press the left button.

Note: To receive messages sent over The Microsoft Network, you must connect to the network. To do so, refer to page 156.

◆ This area displays a list of all your messages. Messages you have not read appear in bold type.

2 To read a message, move the mouse ⇖ over the message and then quickly press the left button twice.

◆ The message appears.

3 When you finish reading the message, move the mouse ⇖ over ⊠ and then press the left button.

After reading a message, you can send a reply. This lets you comment on the message or answer questions.

REPLY TO A MESSAGE

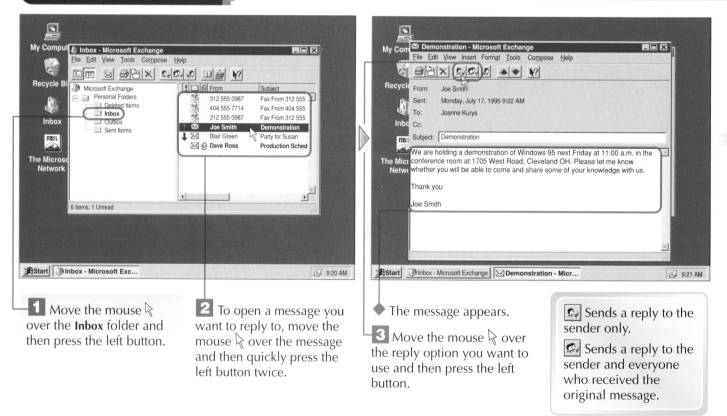

1 Move the mouse ⌖ over the **Inbox** folder and then press the left button.

2 To open a message you want to reply to, move the mouse ⌖ over the message and then quickly press the left button twice.

◆ The message appears.

3 Move the mouse ⌖ over the reply option you want to use and then press the left button.

🔹 Sends a reply to the sender only.

🔹 Sends a reply to the sender and everyone who received the original message.

- Add Name to Address Book
- Send a Message
- Insert a File in a Message
- Delete a Message

- Read a Message
- **Reply to a Message**
- Forward a Message

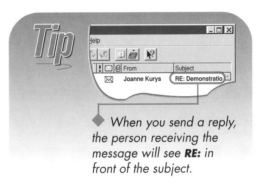

◆ When you send a reply, the person receiving the message will see **RE:** in front of the subject.

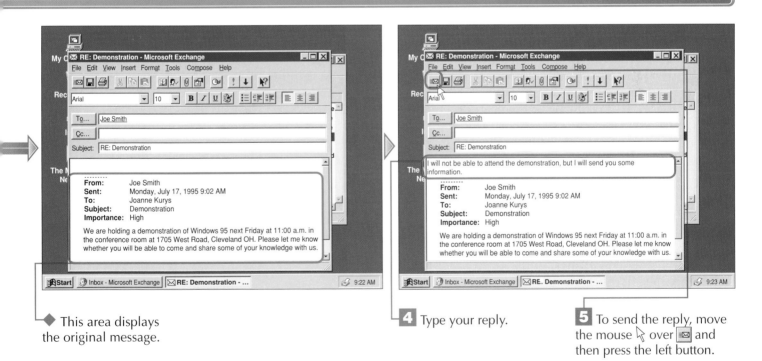

◆ This area displays the original message.

4 Type your reply.

5 To send the reply, move the mouse ⫯ over ▣ and then press the left button.

Note: If you are sending the message over The Microsoft Network, you must connect to the network. To do so, refer to page 156.

FORWARD A MESSAGE

After reading a message, you can add comments and then forward the message to a colleague.

FORWARD A MESSAGE

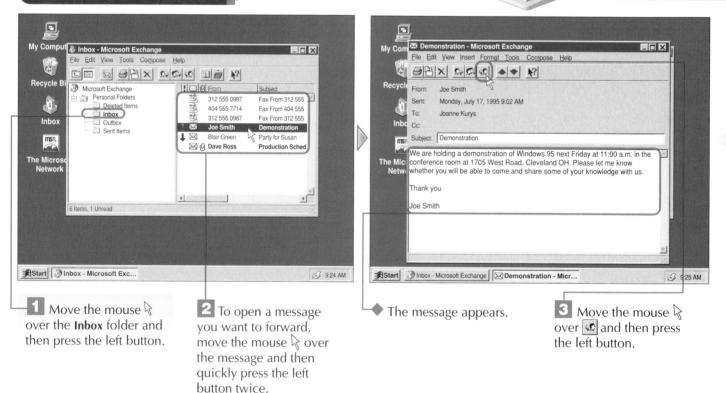

1 Move the mouse ▹ over the **Inbox** folder and then press the left button.

2 To open a message you want to forward, move the mouse ▹ over the message and then quickly press the left button twice.

◆ The message appears.

3 Move the mouse ▹ over 🔧 and then press the left button.

- Add Name to Address Book
- Send a Message
- Insert a File in a Message
- Delete a Message
- Read a Message
- Reply to a Message
- **Forward a Message**

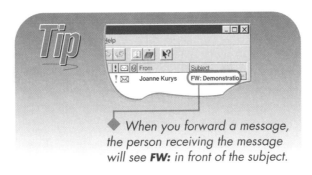

◆ When you forward a message, the person receiving the message will see **FW:** in front of the subject.

◆ This area displays the original message.

4 To specify the person you want to forward the message to, perform steps **2** to **7** starting on page 164.

5 To add your own comments to the message, move the mouse I over this area and then press the left button. Then type your comments.

6 To send the message, move the mouse over ⊠ and then press the left button.

Note: If you are sending the message over The Microsoft Network, you must connect to the network. To do so, refer to page 156.

MAINTAIN YOUR COMPUTER

Format a Disk

Detect and Repair Disk Errors

Defragment a Disk

FORMAT A DISK

You must format a floppy disk before you can use it to store information.

FORMAT A DISK

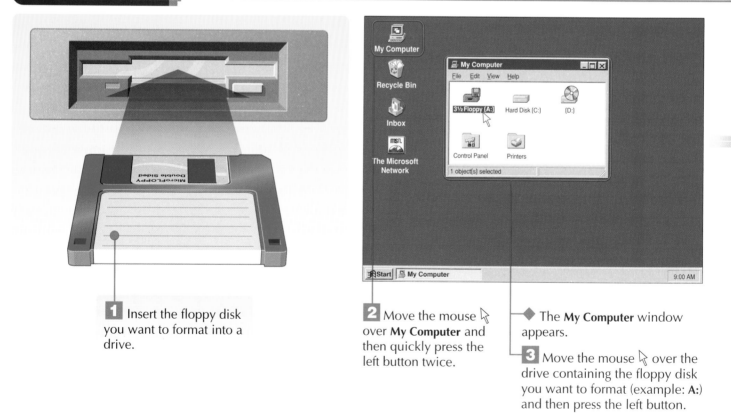

1 Insert the floppy disk you want to format into a drive.

2 Move the mouse ⌖ over **My Computer** and then quickly press the left button twice.

◆ The **My Computer** window appears.

3 Move the mouse ⌖ over the drive containing the floppy disk you want to format (example: **A:**) and then press the left button.

- **Format a Disk**
- Detect and Repair Disk Errors
- Defragment a Disk

IMPORTANT!

Before formatting a floppy disk, make sure the disk does not contain information you want to keep. Formatting will remove all the information on the disk.

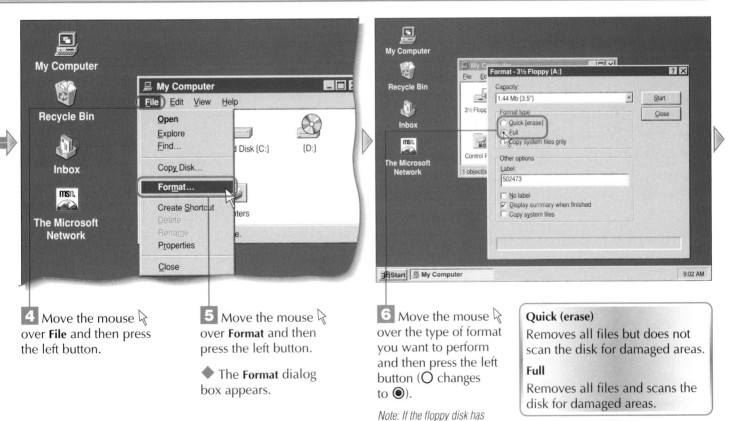

4 Move the mouse ⟍ over **File** and then press the left button.

5 Move the mouse ⟍ over **Format** and then press the left button.

◆ The **Format** dialog box appears.

6 Move the mouse ⟍ over the type of format you want to perform and then press the left button (○ changes to ◉).

*Note: If the floppy disk has never been formatted, select the **Full** option.*

Quick (erase)

Removes all files but does not scan the disk for damaged areas.

Full

Removes all files and scans the disk for damaged areas.

CONTINUED

FORMAT A DISK

> When formatting a floppy disk, you must tell Windows how much information the disk can hold.

DOUBLE-DENSITY 720 Kb

A 3.5 inch floppy disk that has one hole holds 720 Kb of information.

HIGH-DENSITY 1.44 Mb

A 3.5 inch floppy disk that has two holes and displays the HD symbol holds 1.44 Mb of information.

FORMAT A DISK (CONTINUED)

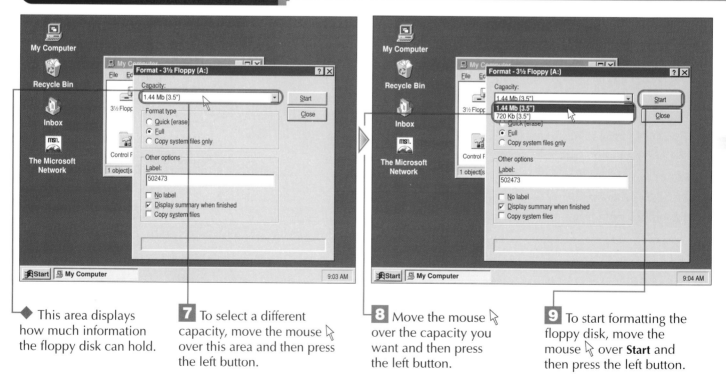

◆ This area displays how much information the floppy disk can hold.

7 To select a different capacity, move the mouse ⟶ over this area and then press the left button.

8 Move the mouse ⟶ over the capacity you want and then press the left button.

9 To start formatting the floppy disk, move the mouse ⟶ over **Start** and then press the left button.

- **Format a Disk**
- Detect and Repair Disk Errors
- Defragment a Disk

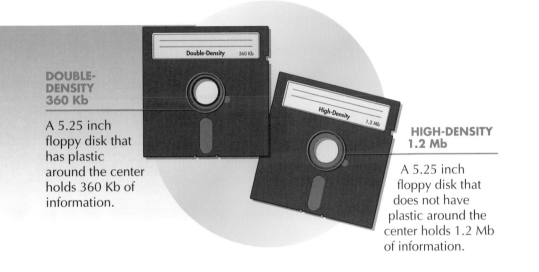

**DOUBLE-
DENSITY
360 Kb**

A 5.25 inch
floppy disk that
has plastic
around the center
holds 360 Kb of
information.

Double-Density 360 Kb

High-Density 1.2 Mb

**HIGH-DENSITY
1.2 Mb**

A 5.25 inch
floppy disk that
does not have
plastic around the
center holds 1.2 Mb
of information.

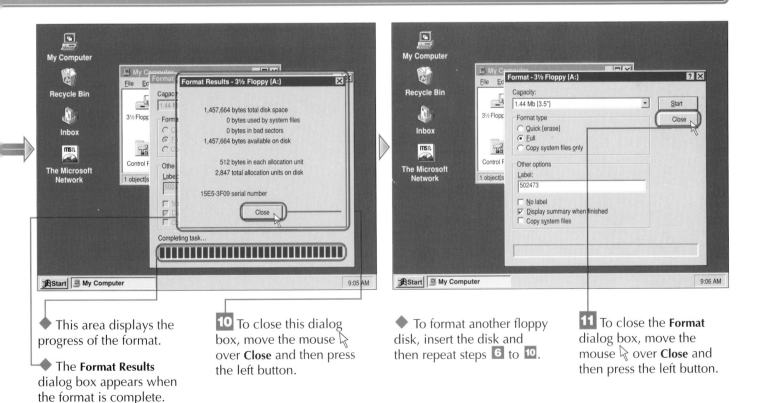

◆ This area displays the
progress of the format.

◆ The **Format Results**
dialog box appears when
the format is complete.
It displays information
about the formatted disk.

10 To close this dialog
box, move the mouse
over **Close** and then press
the left button.

◆ To format another floppy
disk, insert the disk and
then repeat steps **6** to **10**.

11 To close the **Format**
dialog box, move the
mouse over **Close** and
then press the left button.

You can improve the performance of your computer by using ScanDisk to search for and repair disk errors.

The hard disk is the primary device that a computer uses to store information.

DETECT AND REPAIR DISK ERRORS

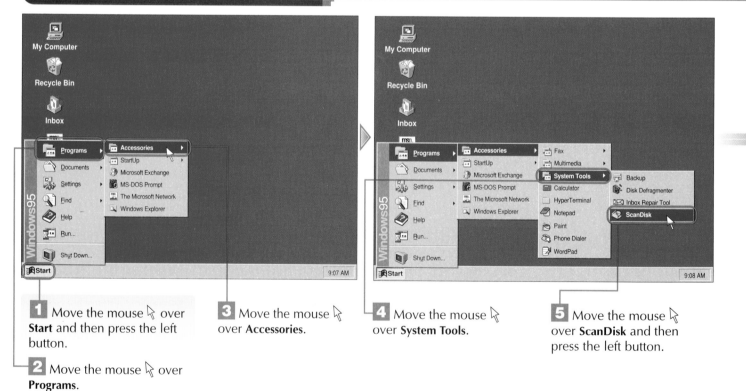

1 Move the mouse ⤢ over **Start** and then press the left button.

2 Move the mouse ⤢ over **Programs**.

3 Move the mouse ⤢ over **Accessories**.

4 Move the mouse ⤢ over **System Tools**.

5 Move the mouse ⤢ over **ScanDisk** and then press the left button.

- Format a Disk
- **Detect and Repair Disk Errors**
- Defragment a Disk

Tip

You should check your hard disk for errors at least once a month.

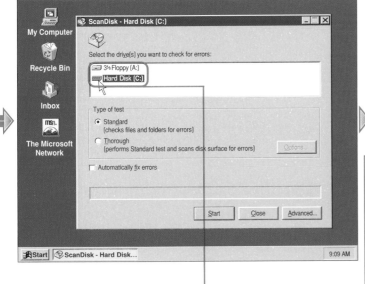

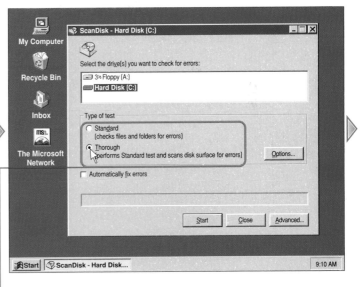

◆ The **ScanDisk** dialog box appears.

6 Move the mouse ⬡ over the drive you want to check for errors (example: **C:**) and then press the left button.

7 Move the mouse ⬡ over the type of test you want to perform (example: **Thorough**) and then press the left button. ○ changes to ◉.

Standard
Checks files and folders for errors.

Thorough
Checks files, folders and the disk surface for errors.

CONTINUED

183

DETECT AND REPAIR DISK ERRORS

You can have Windows automatically repair any disk errors it finds.

8 If you want Windows to automatically repair any disk errors it finds, move the mouse ⫷ over this option and then press the left button (☐ changes to ☑).

9 To start the check, move the mouse ⫷ over **Start** and then press the left button.

◆ This area displays the progress of the check.

- Format a Disk
- **Detect and Repair Disk Errors**
- Defragment a Disk

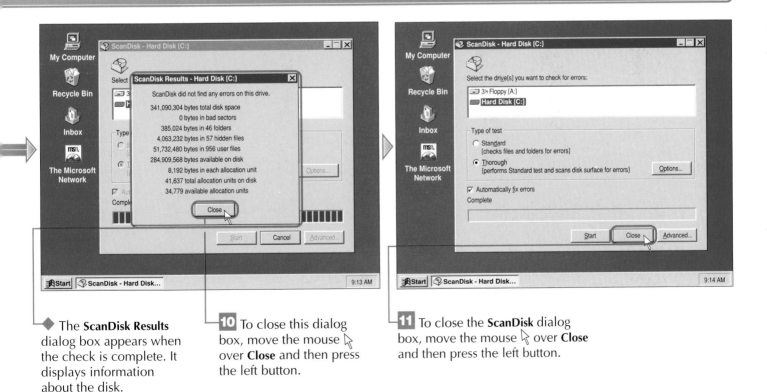

Tip

If you did not tell Windows to automatically repair any disk errors it finds, this dialog box will appear each time ScanDisk finds an error.

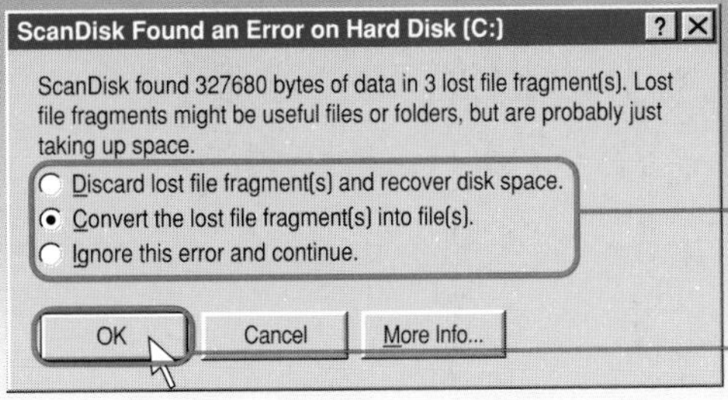

ScanDisk Found an Error on Hard Disk (C:)

ScanDisk found 327680 bytes of data in 3 lost file fragment(s). Lost file fragments might be useful files or folders, but are probably just taking up space.

- ○ Discard lost file fragment(s) and recover disk space.
- ● Convert the lost file fragment(s) into file(s).
- ○ Ignore this error and continue.

OK   Cancel   More Info...

1 To specify how you want to repair the error, move the mouse � over the option you want to use and then press the left button.

2 Move the mouse � over **OK** and then press the left button.

◆ The **ScanDisk Results** dialog box appears when the check is complete. It displays information about the disk.

10 To close this dialog box, move the mouse � over **Close** and then press the left button.

11 To close the **ScanDisk** dialog box, move the mouse � over **Close** and then press the left button.

DEFRAGMENT A DISK

A fragmented hard disk stores parts of a file in many different locations. To retrieve a file, the computer must search many areas on the disk.

DEFRAGMENT A DISK

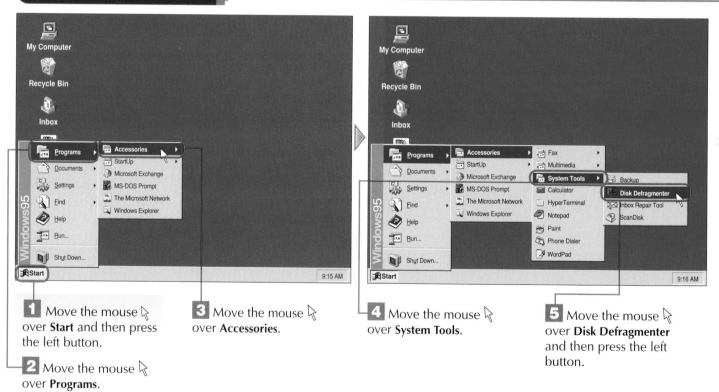

1 Move the mouse ⟍ over **Start** and then press the left button.

2 Move the mouse ⟍ over **Programs**.

3 Move the mouse ⟍ over **Accessories**.

4 Move the mouse ⟍ over **System Tools**.

5 Move the mouse ⟍ over **Disk Defragmenter** and then press the left button.

- Format a Disk
- Detect and Repair Disk Errors
- **Defragment a Disk**

You can improve the performance of your computer by using the Disk Defragmenter program.

You can use the Disk Defragmenter program to place all the parts of a file in one location. This reduces the time the computer will spend locating the file.

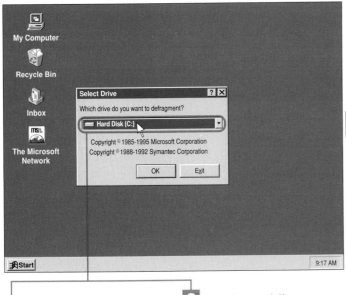

◆ This area displays the drive that Windows will defragment.

6 To select a different drive, move the mouse ⍺ over this area and then press the left button.

◆ A list of the drives on your computer appears.

7 Move the mouse ⍺ over the drive you want to defragment (example: **C:**) and then press the left button.

8 Move the mouse ⍺ over **OK** and then press the left button.

CONTINUED

DEFRAGMENT A DISK

You can perform other tasks on your computer while Windows defragments a disk, but your computer will operate slower.

PRINTING...

DEFRAGMENT A DISK (CONTINUED)

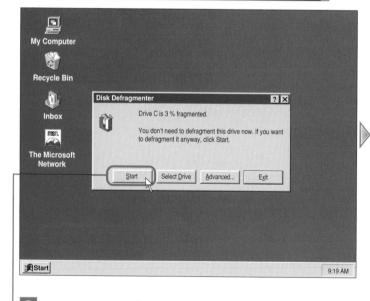

9 Move the mouse ⬦ over **Start** and then press the left button.

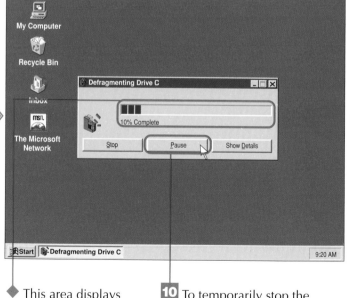

◆ This area displays the progress of the defragmentation.

10 To temporarily stop the defragmentation so you can perform other tasks at full speed, move the mouse ⬦ over **Pause** and then press the left button.

- Format a Disk
- Detect and Repair Disk Errors
- **Defragment a Disk**

Tip

You should defragment your hard disk at least once a month.

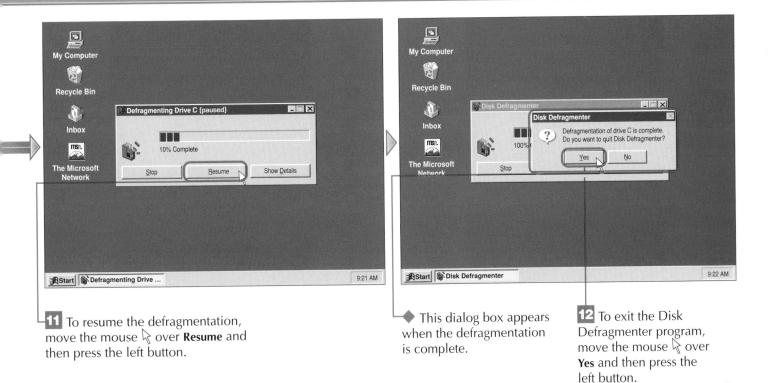

11 To resume the defragmentation, move the mouse ⤷ over **Resume** and then press the left button.

◆ This dialog box appears when the defragmentation is complete.

12 To exit the Disk Defragmenter program, move the mouse ⤷ over **Yes** and then press the left button.

189

BACK UP YOUR FILES

In this chapter you will learn how to make backup copies of files stored on your computer.

BACKUP DEVICES

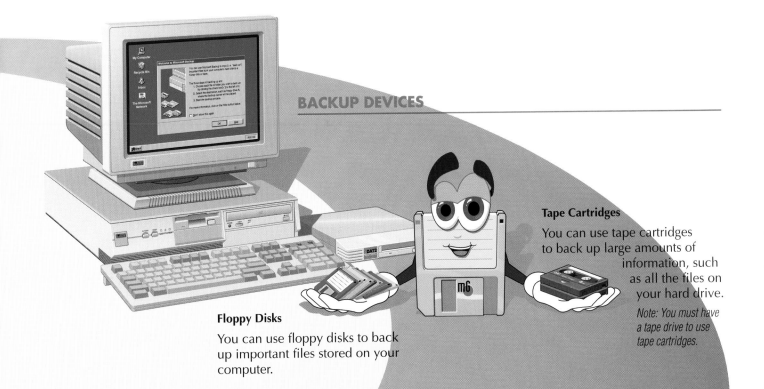

Floppy Disks

You can use floppy disks to back up important files stored on your computer.

Tape Cartridges

You can use tape cartridges to back up large amounts of information, such as all the files on your hard drive.

Note: You must have a tape drive to use tape cartridges.

BACKUP STRATEGIES

Back up your work frequently. Consider how much work you can afford to lose. If you cannot afford to lose the work accomplished in one day, back up once a day. If your work does not change much during the week, back up once a week.

Create and then strictly follow a backup schedule. Hard drive disasters always seem to happen right after you miss a scheduled backup.

Minimize your chances of losing important information by making at least two sets of backup copies. Keep one set near your computer and the second set in another building.

Store backup copies in a cool, dry place, away from electrical equipment and magnetic devices.

START MICROSOFT BACKUP

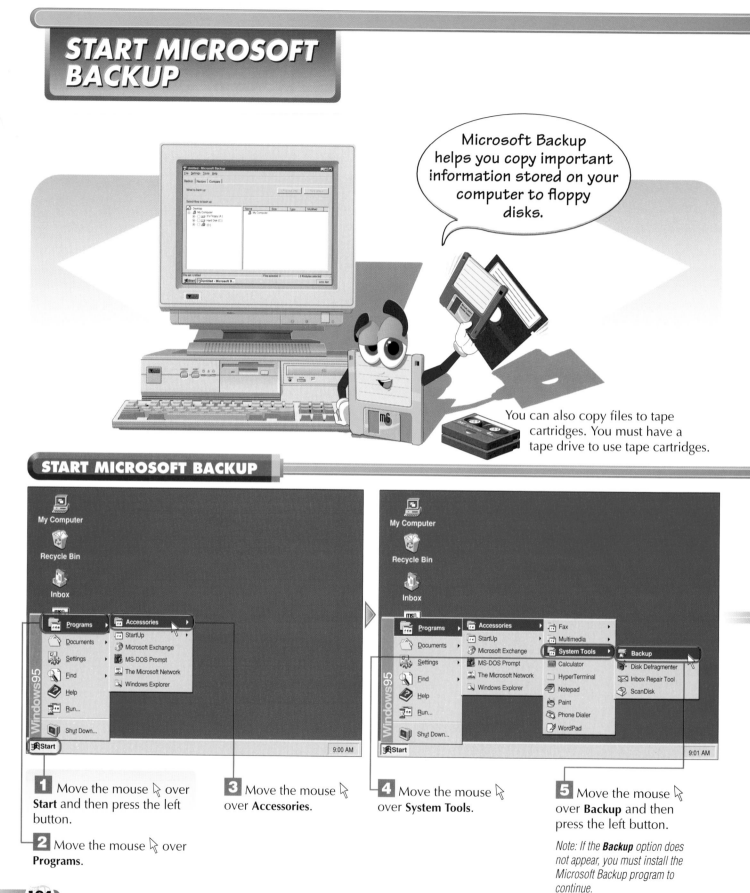

Microsoft Backup helps you copy important information stored on your computer to floppy disks.

You can also copy files to tape cartridges. You must have a tape drive to use tape cartridges.

START MICROSOFT BACKUP

1 Move the mouse ⫯ over **Start** and then press the left button.

2 Move the mouse ⫯ over **Programs**.

3 Move the mouse ⫯ over **Accessories**.

4 Move the mouse ⫯ over **System Tools**.

5 Move the mouse ⫯ over **Backup** and then press the left button.

*Note: If the **Backup** option does not appear, you must install the Microsoft Backup program to continue.*

- Introduction
- **Start Microsoft Backup**
- Back Up Selected Files
- Perform the Backup
- Back Up Named Files
- Restore Files

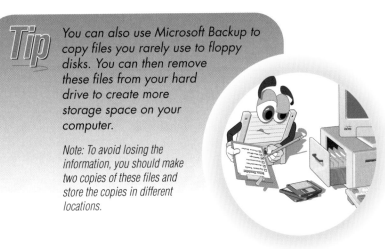

Tip

You can also use Microsoft Backup to copy files you rarely use to floppy disks. You can then remove these files from your hard drive to create more storage space on your computer.

Note: To avoid losing the information, you should make two copies of these files and store the copies in different locations.

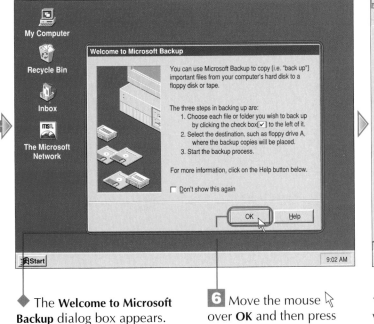

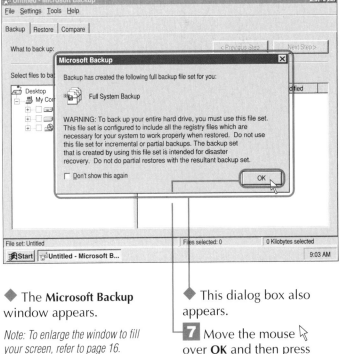

◆ The **Welcome to Microsoft Backup** dialog box appears.

6 Move the mouse ⬚ over **OK** and then press the left button.

◆ The **Microsoft Backup** window appears.

Note: To enlarge the window to fill your screen, refer to page 16.

◆ This dialog box also appears.

7 Move the mouse ⬚ over **OK** and then press the left button.

To perform a backup, you must select the files you want to back up.

BACKUP BASKET

BACK UP SELECTED FILES

◆ To start **Microsoft Backup**, refer to page 194.

1 Move the mouse ⍟ over the plus sign (⊞) beside the drive containing the files you want to back up and then press the left button.

◆ The folders on the drive you selected appear.

◆ A plus sign (⊞) beside a folder indicates that the folders it contains are hidden.

2 To display the hidden folders within a folder, move the mouse ⍟ over the plus sign (⊞) beside the folder and then press the left button.

- Introduction
- Start Microsoft Backup
- **Back Up Selected Files**
- Perform the Backup
- Back Up Named Files
- Restore Files

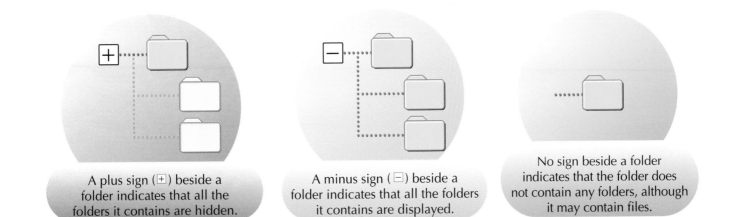

A plus sign (⊞) beside a folder indicates that all the folders it contains are hidden.

A minus sign (⊟) beside a folder indicates that all the folders it contains are displayed.

No sign beside a folder indicates that the folder does not contain any folders, although it may contain files.

◆ The hidden folders appear.

3 To display the contents of a folder, move the mouse ⇙ over the name of the folder and then press the left button.

◆ This area displays the contents of the folder you selected.

4 To back up the files in a folder, move the mouse ⇙ over the box (☐) beside the folder and then press the left button. ☐ changes to ☑.

◆ To back up a specific file, move the mouse ⇙ over the box (☐) beside the file and then press the left button. Repeat this for each file you want to back up.

5 Repeat steps **2** to **4** until you have selected all the files you want to back up.

CONTINUED

If you often back up the same files, you can assign a name to the group of files. This saves you time in future backups.

BACK UP SELECTED FILES (CONTINUED)

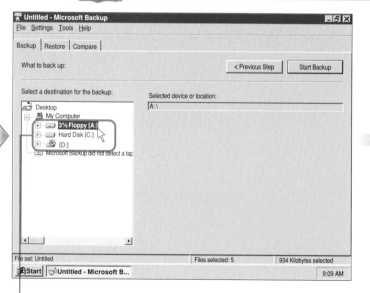

◆ This area displays the number and total size of the files you selected.

6 Move the mouse ⮕ over **Next Step** and then press the left button.

7 Move the mouse ⮕ over the drive where you want to copy the files (example: **A:**) and then press the left button.

- Introduction
- Start Microsoft Backup
- **Back Up Selected Files**
- Perform the Backup
- Back Up Named Files
- Restore Files

Bytes are used to measure the size of files.

One byte equals one character.

Note: A character can be a number, letter or symbol.

One kilobyte equals approximately one thousand characters, or one page of double spaced text.

Note: If your files total more than 5000 kilobytes, you should use a tape cartridge to back up the files.

8 To name the group of files you selected, move the mouse over **File** and then press the left button.

9 Move the mouse over **Save As** and then press the left button.

◆ The **Save As** dialog box appears.

10 Type a name for the group of files.

11 Move the mouse over **Save** and then press the left button.

Note: To perform the backup, refer to page 200.

After you have selected the files you want to back up, you can have Windows copy the files to floppy disks.

PERFORM THE BACKUP

1 Insert a floppy disk into a floppy drive.

2 Move the mouse over **Start Backup** and then press the left button.

3 Type a name for the backup.

Note: To make it easier to identify the backup later, you can name the backup with the current date.

4 Move the mouse over **OK** and then press the left button.

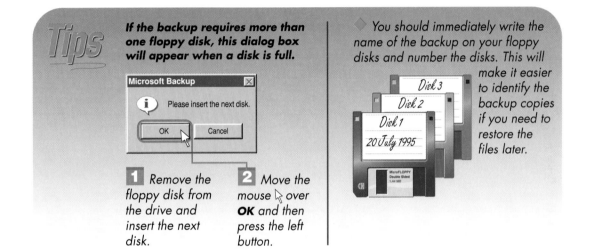

Tips

If the backup requires more than one floppy disk, this dialog box will appear when a disk is full.

Microsoft Backup

ⓘ Please insert the next disk.

OK   Cancel

◆ You should immediately write the name of the backup on your floppy disks and number the disks. This will make it easier to identify the backup copies if you need to restore the files later.

Disk 3
Disk 2
Disk 1
20 July 1995

MicroFLOPPY
Double Sided
1.44 MB

1 Remove the floppy disk from the drive and insert the next disk.

2 Move the mouse ⍫ over **OK** and then press the left button.

◆ This dialog box appears when the backup is complete.

5 To close the dialog box, move the mouse ⍫ over **OK** and then press the left button.

6 To return to the **Microsoft Backup** window, move the mouse ⍫ over **OK** and then press the left button.

7 To close the **Microsoft Backup** window, move the mouse ⍫ over **☒** and then press the left button.

BACK UP NAMED FILES

> If you assigned a name to a group of files in a previous backup, Windows can save you time by selecting those files for you.

BACK UP

Important files

BACK UP NAMED FILES

◆ To start **Microsoft Backup**, refer to page 194.

1 Move the mouse ⬧ over **File** and then press the left button.

2 Move the mouse ⬧ over **Open File Set** and then press the left button.

◆ The **Open** dialog box appears.

3 Move the mouse ⬧ over the name of the group of files you want to back up and then press the left button.

4 Move the mouse ⬧ over **Open** and then press the left button.

- Introduction
- Start Microsoft Backup
- Back Up Selected Files
- Perform the Backup
- **Back Up Named Files**
- Restore Files

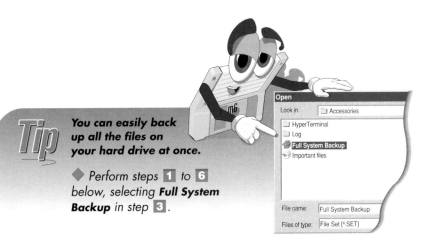

Tip

You can easily back up all the files on your hard drive at once.

◆ Perform steps **1** to **6** below, selecting **Full System Backup** in step **3**.

---

5 Move the mouse ⤢ over **Next Step** and then press the left button.

6 Move the mouse ⤢ over the drive where you want to copy the files (example: **A:**) and then press the left button.

Note: To perform the backup, refer to page 200.

RESTORE FILES

If files on your computer are lost or damaged, you can use your backup copies to restore the files.

RESTORE FILES

1 Start the **Microsoft Backup** program.

Note: To start Microsoft Backup, refer to page 194.

2 Move the mouse ⬡ over the **Restore** tab and then press the left button.

3 Insert the floppy disk that contains the files you want to restore into a drive.

4 Move the mouse ⬡ over the drive that contains the floppy disk (example: **A:**) and then press the left button.

IMPORTANT!

If your backup copies are stored on more than one floppy disk, you must insert the **last** disk in step **3** below.

5 Move the mouse ▷ over the name of the backup you want to restore and then press the left button.

6 Move the mouse ▷ over **Next Step** and then press the left button.

◆ This area displays the folders from the backup you selected.

7 To display the contents of a folder, move the mouse ▷ over the name of the folder and then press the left button.

◆ The contents of the folder you selected appear.

CONTINUED

RESTORE FILES

If you do not need to restore all the files you backed up, you can select only the files you want to restore.

RESTORE FILES (CONTINUED)

8 To restore all the files in a folder, move the mouse ⇗ over the box (☐) beside the folder and then press the left button. ☐ changes to ☑.

◆ To restore a specific file, move the mouse ⇗ over the box (☐) beside the file and then press the left button. Repeat this for each file you want to restore.

9 Repeat steps **7** and **8** until you have selected all the files you want to restore.

◆ This area displays the number and total size of the files you selected.

*Note: If your backup copies are stored on more than one floppy disk, insert the **first** disk into the drive.*

10 Move the mouse ⇗ over **Start Restore** and then press the left button.

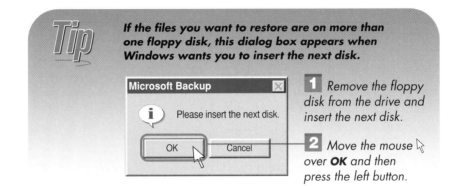

Tip

If the files you want to restore are on more than one floppy disk, this dialog box appears when Windows wants you to insert the next disk.

1 *Remove the floppy disk from the drive and insert the next disk.*

2 *Move the mouse over **OK** and then press the left button.*

◆ This dialog box appears when the files are restored.

11 Move the mouse over **OK** and then press the left button.

12 To return to the **Microsoft Backup** window, move the mouse over **OK** and then press the left button.

13 To close the **Microsoft Backup** window, move the mouse over ☒ and then press the left button.

INDEX

A

active window, 22
address book, adding names to, 162–163
aligning text, 51
arranging icons, 76–77
arranging windows, 24–25

B

backup. *See* Microsoft Backup
    devices and strategies, 193
bold option, 50
Bulletin Board Services (BBS), 155

C

cascading windows, 24
Categories, The Microsoft Network, 157
CD-ROM (D:), 71
centering text, 51
clicking, with mouse, 7
closing windows, 27
colors, changing for screen, 130–131
copying
    files to floppy disks, 90–91
    files to folders, 89, 121
    folders, 91
    text in WordPad documents, 49
cover pages for faxes, 144
Ctrl+A, selecting all text in documents with, 43

D

date
    changing, 126–127
    displaying on screen, 9
defragmenting disks, 186–189
deleting
    e-mail messages, 170
    files and folders, 102–103, 122–123
    parts of Paint drawings, 60–61
    text in WordPad documents, 47
desktop, 8
    adding shortcut icons to, 110–111
    creating folders on, 87
    renaming files and folders on, 92–93
disk errors, detecting and repairing, 182–185
disks
    defragmenting, 186–189
    detecting and repairing errors in, 182–185
    formatting, 178–181
    sizes and capacities of, 180–181
    using for backups. *See* Microsoft Backup
displaying and hiding folders, 117
documents. *See* WordPad
double-clicking, 7
    changing speed of, 136
drag and drop, 7
drawing
    lines in Paint, 56–57
    shapes in Paint, 58–59
drawings. *See* Paint
drives, 70–71
    displaying contents of , 72–73

E

editing text in WordPad documents, 46–47
electronic mail. *See* e-mail
e-mail, 140, 154, 157
    address books, 165
    deleting messages, 170
    forwarding messages, 174–175
    inserting files in messages, 168–169
    Microsoft Network, The, 154, 157
    reading, 171
    replying to, 172–173
    sending messages, 164–167
    symbols, 171
erasing areas in Paint drawings, 60–61
exiting
    Microsoft Backup, 201, 207
    Microsoft Network, The, 159
    Paint, 65
    Windows, 12–13
    WordPad, 39
Explorer. *See* Windows Explorer

INDEX

Title	Author	ISBN #	Price
INTERNET/COMMUNICATIONS/NETWORKING			
CompuServe For Dummies™	by Wallace Wang	ISBN: 1-56884-181-7	$19.95 USA/$26.95 Canada
Modems For Dummies™, 2nd Edition	by Tina Rathbone	ISBN: 1-56884-223-6	$19.99 USA/$26.99 Canada
Modems For Dummies™	by Tina Rathbone	ISBN: 1-56884-001-2	$19.95 USA/$26.95 Canada
MORE Internet For Dummies™	by John Levine & Margaret Levine Young	ISBN: 1-56884-164-7	$19.95 USA/$26.95 Canada
NetWare For Dummies™	by Ed Tittel & Deni Connor	ISBN: 1-56884-003-9	$19.95 USA/$26.95 Canada
Networking For Dummies™	by Doug Lowe	ISBN: 1-56884-079-9	$19.95 USA/$26.95 Canada
ProComm Plus 2 For Windows For Dummies™	by Wallace Wang	ISBN: 1-56884-219-8	$19.99 USA/$26.99 Canada
The Internet Help Desk For Dummies™	by John Kaufeld	ISBN: 1-56884-238-4	$16.99 USA/$22.99 Canada
The3 Internet For Dummies™, 2nd Edition	by John Levine & Carol Baroudi	ISBN: 1-56884-222-8	$19.99 USA/$26.99 Canada
The Internet For Macs For Dummies™	by Charles Seiter	ISBN: 1-56884-184-1	$19.95 USA/$26.95 Canada
MACINTOSH			
Mac Programming For Dummies™	by Dan Parks Sydow	ISBN: 1-56884-173-6	$19.95 USA/$26.95 Canada
Macintosh System 7.5 For Dummies™	by Bob LeVitus	ISBN: 1-56884-197-3	$19.95 USA/$26.95 Canada
MORE Macs For Dummies™	by David Pogue	ISBN: 1-56884-087-X	$19.95 USA/$26.95 Canada
PageMaker 5 For Macs For Dummies™	by Galen Gruman & Deke McClelland	ISBN: 1-56884-178-7	$19.95 USA/$26.95 Canada
QuarkXPress 3.3 For Dummies™	by Galen Gruman & Barbara Assadi	ISBN: 1-56884-217-1	$19.99 USA/$26.99 Canada
Upgrading and Fixing Macs For Dummies™	by Kearney Rietmann & Frank Higgins	ISBN: 1-56884-189-2	$19.95 USA/$26.95 Canada
MULTIMEDIA			
Multimedia & CD-ROMs For Dummies™, Interactive Multimedia Value Pack	by Andy Rathbone	ISBN: 1-56884-225-2	$29.95 USA/$39.95 Canada
Multimedia & CD-ROMs For Dummies™	by Andy Rathbone	ISBN: 1-56884-089-6	$19.95 USA/$26.95 Canada
OPERATING SYSTEMS/DOS			
MORE DOS For Dummies™	by Dan Gookin	ISBN: 1-56884-046-2	$19.95 USA/$26.95 Canada
S.O.S. For DOS™	by Katherine Murray	ISBN: 1-56884-043-8	$12.95 USA/$16.95 Canada
OS/2 For Dummies™	by Andy Rathbone	ISBN: 1-878058-76-2	$19.95 USA/$26.95 Canada
UNIX			
UNIX For Dummies™	by John Levine & Margaret Levine Young	ISBN: 1-878058-58-4	$19.95 USA/$26.95 Canada
WINDOWS			
S.O.S. For Windows™	by Katherine Murray	ISBN: 1-56884-045-4	$12.95 USA/$16.95 Canada
Windows "X" For Dummies™, 3rd Edition	by Andy Rathbone	ISBN: 1-56884-240-6	$19.99 USA/$26.99 Canada
PCS/HARDWARE			
Illustrated Computer Dictionary For Dummies™	by Dan Gookin, Wally Wang, & Chris Van Buren	ISBN: 1-56884-004-7	$12.95 USA/$16.95 Canada
Upgrading and Fixing PCs For Dummies™	by Andy Rathbone	ISBN: 1-56884-002-0	$19.95 USA/$26.95 Canada
PRESENTATION/AUTOCAD			
AutoCAD For Dummies™	by Bud Smith	ISBN: 1-56884-191-4	$19.95 USA/$26.95 Canada
PowerPoint 4 For Windows For Dummies™	by Doug Lowe	ISBN: 1-56884-161-2	$16.95 USA/$22.95 Canada
PROGRAMMING			
Borland C++ For Dummies™	by Michael Hyman	ISBN: 1-56884-162-0	$19.95 USA/$26.95 Canada
"Borland's New Language Product" For Dummies™	by Neil Rubenking	ISBN: 1-56884-200-7	$19.95 USA/$26.95 Canada
C For Dummies™	by Dan Gookin	ISBN: 1-878058-78-9	$19.95 USA/$26.95 Canada
C++ For Dummies™	by S. Randy Davis	ISBN: 1-56884-163-9	$19.95 USA/$26.95 Canada
Mac Programming For Dummies™	by Dan Parks Sydow	ISBN: 1-56884-173-6	$19.95 USA/$26.95 Canada
QBasic Programming For Dummies™	by Douglas Hergert	ISBN: 1-56884-093-4	$19.95 USA/$26.95 Canada
Visual Basic "X" For Dummies™, 2nd Edition	by Wallace Wang	ISBN: 1-56884-230-9	$19.99 USA/$26.99 Canada
Visual Basic 3 For Dummies™	by Wallace Wang	ISBN: 1-56884-076-4	$19.95 USA/$26.95 Canada
SPREADSHEET			
1-2-3 For Dummies™	by Greg Harvey	ISBN: 1-878058-60-6	$16.95 USA/$22.95 Canada
1-2-3 For Windows 5 For Dummies™, 2nd Edition	by John Walkenbach	ISBN: 1-56884-216-3	$16.95 USA/$22.95 Canada
1-2-3 For Windows For Dummies™	by John Walkenbach	ISBN: 1-56884-052-7	$16.95 USA/$22.95 Canada
Excel 5 For Macs For Dummies™	by Greg Harvey	ISBN: 1-56884-186-8	$19.95 USA/$26.95 Canada
Excel For Dummies™, 2nd Edition	by Greg Harvey	ISBN: 1-56884-050-0	$16.95 USA/$22.95 Canada
MORE Excel 5 For Windows For Dummies™	by Greg Harvey	ISBN: 1-56884-207-4	$19.95 USA/$26.95 Canada
Quattro Pro 6 For Windows For Dummies™	by John Walkenbach	ISBN: 1-56884-174-4	$19.95 USA/$26.95 Canada
Quattro Pro For DOS For Dummies™	by John Walkenbach	ISBN: 1-56884-023-3	$16.95 USA/$22.95 Canada
UTILITIES			
Norton Utilities 8 For Dummies™	by Beth Slick	ISBN: 1-56884-166-3	$19.95 USA/$26.95 Canada
VCRS/CAMCORDERS			
VCRs & Camcorders For Dummies™	by Andy Rathbone & Gordon McComb	ISBN: 1-56884-229-5	$14.99 USA/$20.99 Canada
WORD PROCESSING			
Ami Pro For Dummies™	by Jim Meade	ISBN: 1-56884-049-7	$19.95 USA/$26.95 Canada
More Word For Windows 6 For Dummies™	by Doug Lowe	ISBN: 1-56884-165-5	$19.95 USA/$26.95 Canada
MORE WordPerfect 6 For Windows For Dummies™	by Margaret Levine Young & David C. Kay	ISBN: 1-56884-206-6	$19.95 USA/$26.95 Canada
MORE WordPerfect 6 For DOS For Dummies™	by Wallace Wang, edited by Dan Gookin	ISBN: 1-56884-047-0	$19.95 USA/$26.95 Canada
S.O.S. For WordPerfect™	by Katherine Murray	ISBN: 1-56884-053-5	$12.95 USA/$16.95 Canada
Word 6 For Macs For Dummies™	by Dan Gookin	ISBN: 1-56884-190-6	$19.95 USA/$26.95 Canada
Word For Windows 6 For Dummies™	by Dan Gookin	ISBN: 1-56884-075-6	$16.95 USA/$22.95 Canada
Word For Windows 2 For Dummies™	by Dan Gookin	ISBN: 1-878058-86-X	$16.95 USA/$22.95 Canada
WordPerfect 6 For Dummies™	by Dan Gookin	ISBN: 1-878058-77-0	$16.95 USA/$22.95 Canada
WordPerfect For Dummies™	by Dan Gookin	ISBN: 1-878058-52-5	$16.95 USA/$22.95 Canada
WordPerfect For Windows For Dummies™	by Margaret Levine Young & David C. Kay	ISBN: 1-56884-032-2	$16.95 USA/$22.95 Canada

IDG's 3-D Visual™ Series

from: **maranGraphics™**

The Proven 3-D Visual Approach to Learning Computers In A Handy **NEW** Pocket Size

Excel 5 For Windows Visual PocketGuide

ISBN 1-56884-667-3
$14.99 USA/£13.99 UK

Windows 3.1 Visual PocketGuide

ISBN 1-56884-650-9
$14.99 USA/£13.99 UK

Word 6 For Windows Visual PocketGuide

ISBN 1-56884-666-5
$14.99 USA/£13.99 UK

Also Available!

Windows 95 Visual PocketGuide

ISBN 1-56884-661-4
$14.99 USA/£13.99 UK

Lotus 1-2-3 R5 For Windows Visual PocketGuide

ISBN 1-56884-671-1
$14.99 USA/£13.99 UK

WordPerfect 6.1 For Windows Visual PocketGuide

ISBN 1-56884-668-1
$14.99 USA/£13.99 UK

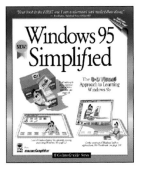

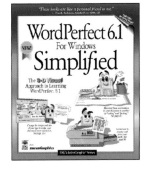
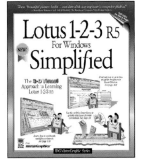

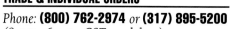

TRADE & INDIVIDUAL ORDERS

Phone: **(800) 762-2974** *or* **(317) 895-5200**
(8 a.m.–6 p.m., CST, weekdays)
FAX : **(317) 895-5298**

CORPORATE ORDERS FOR 3-D VISUAL™ SERIES

Phone: **(800) 469-6616** *ext.* **206**
(8 a.m.–5 p.m., EST, weekdays)
FAX : **(905) 890-9434**

IDG BOOKS

***maranGraphics*™**

Qty	ISBN	Title	Price	Total

Shipping & Handling Charges

	Description	First book	Each add'l. book	Total
Domestic	Normal	$4.50	$1.50	$
	Two Day Air	$8.50	$2.50	$
	Overnight	$18.00	$3.00	$
International	Surface	$8.00	$8.00	$
	Airmail	$16.00	$16.00	$
	DHL Air	$17.00	$17.00	$

Subtotal _____

*CA residents add
applicable sales tax* _____

*IN, MA and MD
residents add
5% sales tax* _____

*IL residents add
6.25% sales tax* _____

*RI residents add
7% sales tax* _____

*TX residents add
8.25% sales tax* _____

Shipping _____

Total _____

Ship to:

Name _____

Address _____

Company _____

City/State/Zip _____

Daytime Phone _____

Payment: ☐ Check to IDG Books (US Funds Only)

☐ Visa   ☐ Mastercard   ☐ American Express

Card # _____ Exp. _____ Signature _____

IDG Books Education Group
Jim Kelly, Director of Education Sales – 9 Village Circle, Ste. 450, Westlake, TX 76262
800-434-2086 Phone • 817-430-5852 Fax • 8:30-5:00 CST

IDG BOOKS WORLDWIDE REGISTRATION CARD

Title of this book: Windows 95 Simplified

My overall rating of this book: ❏ Very good [1] ❏ Good [2] ❏ Satisfactory [3] ❏ Fair [4] ❏ Poor [5]

How I first heard about this book:

❏ Found in bookstore; name: [6]   ❏ Book review: [7]

❏ Advertisement: [8]   ❏ Catalog: [9]

❏ Word of mouth; heard about book from friend, co-worker, etc.: [10]   ❏ Other: [11]

What I liked most about this book:

What I would change, add, delete, etc., in future editions of this book:

Other comments:

Number of computer books I purchase in a year: ❏ 1 [12] ❏ 2-5 [13] ❏ 6-10 [14] ❏ More than 10 [15]

I would characterize my computer skills as: ❏ Beginner [16] ❏ Intermediate [17] ❏ Advanced [18] ❏ Professional [19]

I use ❏ DOS [20] ❏ Windows [21] ❏ OS/2 [22] ❏ Unix [23] ❏ Macintosh [24] ❏ Other: [25]_____
(please specify)

I would be interested in new books on the following subjects:
(please check all that apply, and use the spaces provided to identify specific software)

❏ Word processing: [26]   ❏ Spreadsheets: [27]

❏ Data bases: [28]   ❏ Desktop publishing: [29]

❏ File Utilities: [30]   ❏ Money management: [31]

❏ Networking: [32]   ❏ Programming languages: [33]

❏ Other: [34]

I use a PC at (please check all that apply): ❏ home [35] ❏ work [36] ❏ school [37] ❏ other: [38] _____

The disks I prefer to use are ❏ 5.25 [39] ❏ 3.5 [40] ❏ other: [41]_____

I have a CD ROM: ❏ yes [42] ❏ no [43]

I plan to buy or upgrade computer hardware this year: ❏ yes [44] ❏ no [45]

I plan to buy or upgrade computer software this year: ❏ yes [46] ❏ no [47]

Name: _____ Business title: [48] _____ Type of Business: [49] _____

Address (❏ home [50] ❏ work [51]/Company name: _____)

Street/Suite#

City [52]/State [53]/Zipcode [54]: _____ Country [55] _____

❏ **I liked this book!** You may quote me by name in future
IDG Books Worldwide promotional materials.

My daytime phone number is _____

IDG BOOKS

THE WORLD OF
COMPUTER
KNOWLEDGE

❏ YES!

Please keep me informed about IDG's World of Computer Knowledge.
Send me the latest IDG Books catalog.